NATURAL WONDERS
OF WASHINGTON

NATURAL WONDERS OF WASHINGTON

Archie Satterfield

COUNTRY ROADS PRESS
Oaks • Pennsylvania

Natural Wonders of Washington:
A Guide to Parks, Preserves & Wild Places

Originally titled *Green Guide to Washington*. Updated, with additional information.

Published by Country Roads Press
P.O. Box 838, 2170 West Drive
Oaks, PA 19456

Text design by Studio 3.
Map by Lois Leonard Stock.
Illustrations by Dale Ingrid Swensson.
Typesetting by Typeworks.

ISBN 1-56626-151-1

Library of Congress Cataloging-in-Publication Data

Satterfield, Archie.
[Green guide, Washington]
Natural wonders of Washington : a guide to parks, preserves and wild places / by Archie Satterfield ; illustrator, Dale Ingrid Swensson.
p. cm.
Previous title: "Green guide to Washington"–CIP data sheet.
Includes bibliographical references and index.
ISBN 1-56626-151-1
1. Washington (State)–Guidebooks. 2. Parks–Washington (State)–Guidebooks. 3. Wildlife refuges–Washington (State)–Guidebooks. 4. National parks and reserves–Washington (State)–Guidebooks. 5. Natural areas–Washington (State)–Guidebooks. 6. Natural history–Washington (State)–Guidebooks. 7. Gardens–Washington (State)–Guidebooks. I. Title.
F889.3.S3 1995
917.9704'43–dc20 95-7204
CIP

Printed in the United States of America.
10 9 8 7 6 5 4 3 2 1

This book is dedicated
to the memory of Nelson Bentley,
one of Washington's finest poets,
who loved nature more than most of us,
was a superb teacher, and most of all
was a kind and decent human being.

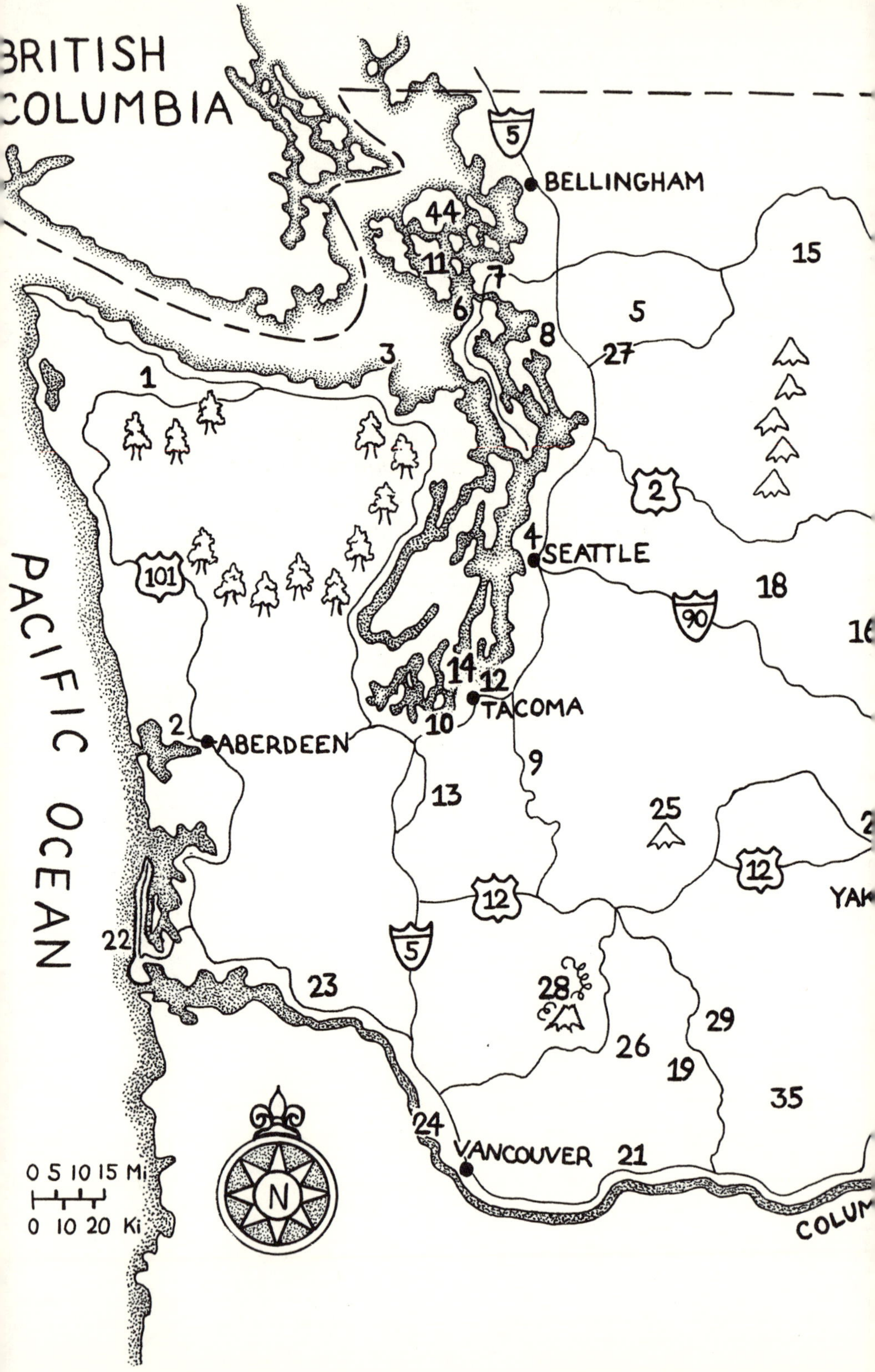
BRITISH COLUMBIA
PACIFIC OCEAN
BELLINGHAM
SEATTLE
TACOMA
ABERDEEN
VANCOUVER
YAK
COLUM
5
101
2
90
12
44
11
7
6
8
3
1
5
27
15
4
18
16
14
12
10
2
9
13
25
22
23
28
26
29
19
35
24
21
0 5 10 15 Mi
0 10 20 Ki
N

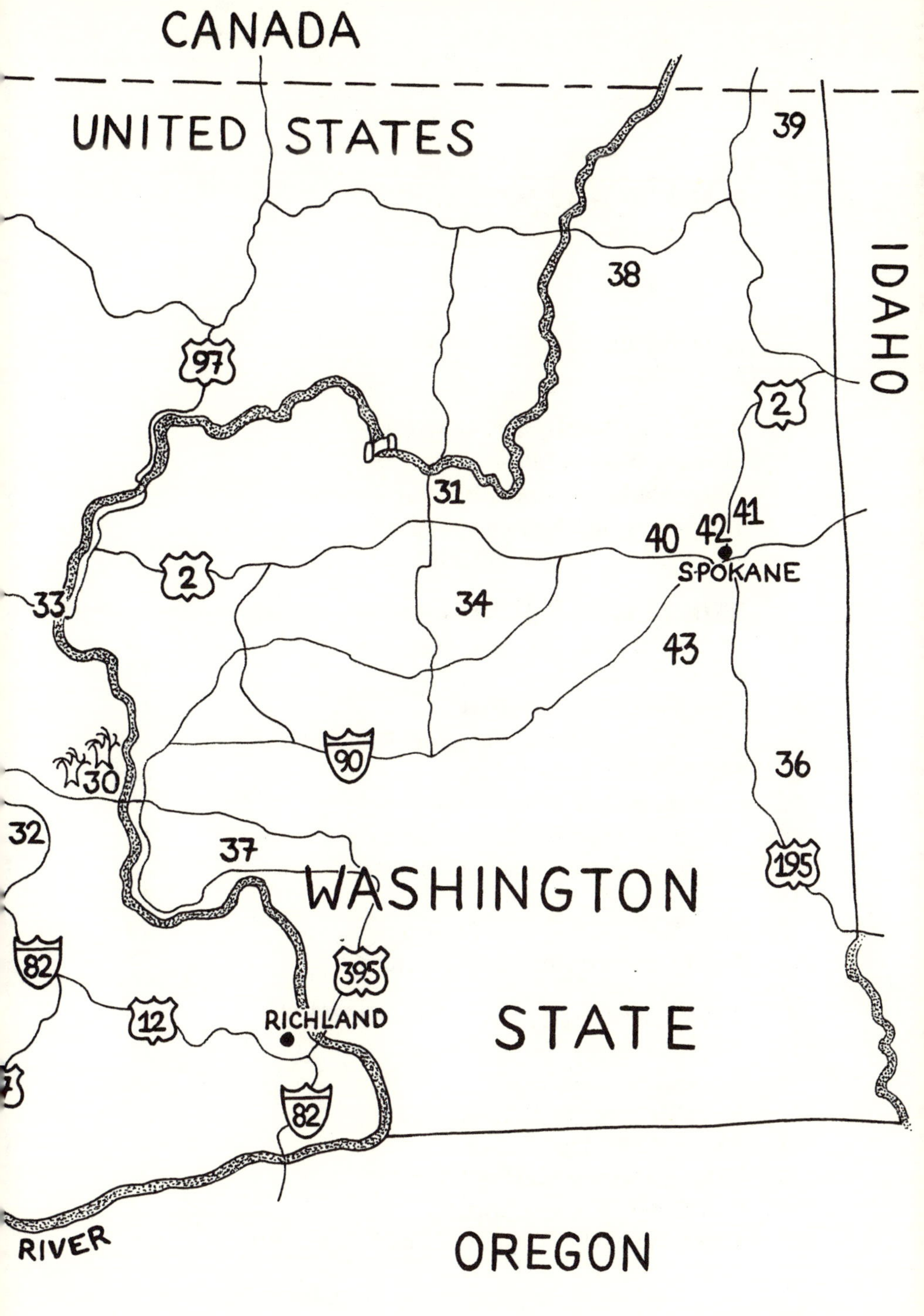
CANADA
UNITED STATES
IDAHO
39
38
97
2
31
40
42
41
SPOKANE
33
2
34
43
90
30
36
32
37
WASHINGTON
STATE
195
82
395
RICHLAND
12
82
RIVER
OREGON

Contents

Acknowledgments

I have relied on the kindness and courtesy of many people while writing this book. Now that it is done, my major worry is being certain to give credit to everyone. I hope the following list is complete. If errors appear, the fault is mine alone.

Gary Yeager of the Spokane office of the U.S. Bureau of Land Management was extremely helpful, as was Al Gilson of the Spokane/Inland Northwest News Bureau. Steve Jenks, fish biologist with the U.S. Department of Fisheries, was prompt in providing materials, as was Jeff Weathersby of the U.S. Department of Wildlife. Cassandra Toney of the Tacoma–Pierce County Visitor and Convention Bureau sent a large and very useful package of materials. Kathleen South of the Point Defiance Zoo and Aquarium was equally helpful. Numerous Forest Service personnel were helpful, some of whom did not include their names with the packages of information they sent. One who did was Maydene Ewer of the Okanogan National Forest.

I also would like to thank the staff of Country Roads Press for their speedy decisions, on-time payments, and courtesy throughout the editing process.

Introduction

Like nearly everyone who likes the outdoors and lives in Washington because it has a lot of wilderness, I spend a lot of time grumbling about the increasing population and the disappearance of wild places. After researching this book, however, I must admit that Washington still has a lot of outdoors left. It is surprising how much wildlife habitat has been saved and how much is in the process of being purchased by various public agencies for preservation.

Washington also is blessed with large national parks. Mount Rainier, Olympic, and North Cascades National Parks are very important to the high quality of life we have come to expect. Added to this is an elaborate system of wildlife refuges throughout the state. Although it is true that you can't eat scenery, as opponents of wilderness areas like to say, it is equally true that these large chunks of natural beauty have other benefits. They create a tourist industry, which ranks either third or fourth as a source of income to the state, and they create something else that can never be translated into dollars: a high quality of life.

For this book, I have selected nearly fifty green places that I think are representative of certain areas. I selected some for no better reason than they are places I happen to like. I have stacks of books, booklets, brochures, and other resources in my files concerning places that didn't make the final cut. To have included them all would have required an encyclopedia. In spite of my worst fears, the state isn't in mortal danger of becoming a gigantic suburb after all. Not yet, anyway.

To help clarify road designations, I've used the following abbreviations: I = interstate, US = U.S. route or highway, and State = state route or highway.

1
The Olympic Peninsula

OLYMPIC NATIONAL PARK

The remote Olympic Peninsula, most of which is preserved by Olympic National Park, is one of the nation's most diverse areas. In only a few miles, the rainfall patterns change from fifteen or more feet a year to less than two feet. The peninsula has one of only three temperate rain forests in the world; the others are in Chile and New Zealand.

The park was created in stages. The first designation was as a forest preserve signed into existence in 1897 by President Grover Cleveland. Then President Theodore Roosevelt got involved and turned 600,000 acres into the Olympic National Monument. But it was the other Roosevelt, President Franklin D., who in 1938 created the park over the objections of many local citizens. In 1953, after another prolonged debate, President Dwight D. Eisenhower added fifty miles of ocean strip to the park.

The peninsula was the last part of Washington to be thoroughly explored. Well into this century, many parts of it had not been seen from the ground. After several scientific expeditions went back into the forests and mountains, they found that the peninsula has four of the seven distinct life zones. No other place in America has so many of these zones, and in no other place in America is a major mountain range so close to an ocean.

The wettest place in the contiguous United States is 7,965-foot Mount Olympus, where the average annual rainfall is 200 inches. This peak also receives the most snow in the contiguous United States.

The national park has ten varieties of wildflowers found nowhere else, and its fifty-seven miles of coastline are the longest stretch of primitive coastline remaining in the contiguous United States. The most famous feature of the park is probably its three rain forests – Quinault, Queets, and Hoh. All are on the western side of the park. They receive about 145 inches of rainfall each year. This large amount of moisture is combined with moderate temperatures that range from a maximum of about 80°F to almost never freezing temperatures.

These temperate rain forests are famous for the dense vegetation that carpets the forest floor. Hardly a square inch of soil isn't covered with some kind of plant life – from microscopic lichens and mosses to evergreen trees more than 300 feet tall. Sitka spruce and western hemlock are the most common species, with Douglas fir, western red cedar, big-leaf maple, vine maple, alder, and black cottonwood are also present.

The visual signature of these rain forests is their mosses, ferns, and lichens. These plants, some of which are parasitic, seem to be everywhere, especially hanging from trees and bushes like green and yellow beards. Fungi also grow from trees here. In addition, the forest floor is covered with fallen trees that have become "nurse logs," sources of food for the next generation of trees and plants.

The sun sometimes works its way down through the

Beautiful but poisonous fly agaric mushroom

canopy sending dramatic rays shooting through the fog and mist. Usually, though, the sky is overcast and the forest rather dark.

The Hoh Rain Forest, the most popular of the three, is the farthest north. You can reach it by turning off US 101 onto the Upper Hoh Road about twelve miles south of Forks. Follow this road east eighteen miles to the Hoh Visitor Center at the entrance to the forest. Two marked trails begin here. The Hall of Mosses Trail is three-quarters of a mile long and passes by many examples of hanging mosses. The Spruce Nature Trail is 1.25 miles long and takes you past many big trees, nurse logs, and, of course, more mosses.

The Queets Rain Forest is at the end of a spur road off US 101 that follows the Queets River inland. Neither it nor the Quinault Rain Forest is as well developed as the Hoh. The Quinault has a one-half-mile trail. The area also has a series of trails unrelated to the rain forest.

Probably the most popular spot in Olympic National

Park is Hurricane Ridge, which has breathtaking views of the entire region, including the Olympic Mountains, the Strait of Juan de Fuca, and Vancouver Island and the Gulf Islands in Canada. The 5,200-foot ridge is at the end of the pleasant seventeen-mile Heart of the Hills Road from Port Angeles that dead-ends on the ridge. The highway has a gradual rise and many turnouts where you can take photographs or pull over in your RV to let the cars behind you pass. At the top is the Hurricane Ridge Lodge, where you can buy food and gifts and participate in naturalist programs.

The view from the ridge is stunning. The lodge has metal maps identifying the mountains spread out before you. Some of the best views are toward the end of the paved trail that leads away from the lodge. All along this route, keep an eye out for deer, black bears, and mountain goats. These goats are not native to the Olympic Peninsula, and they have been bad news ever since they were introduced. They have been grazing vegetation down to the bare ground, creating soil erosion, and there has been much talk about removing them from the area.

Not far from Hurricane Ridge and a few miles west of Port Angeles is Lake Crescent, one of my favorite lakes. Although US 101 runs along its southern shore, Lake Crescent remains one of the most beautiful lakes in the state. It is surrounded by mountains that give the lake a secluded feeling in spite of the highway going by.

Another unusual place is Cape Alava on the northern end of Olympic National Park's coastal strip. A major archaeological dig was conducted here several years ago to unearth Ozette, a Native American village that had been buried centuries before by a mud slide. The village was situated in a sheltered but very rocky area, an excellent place for the Native Americans to launch their boats and hunt sea mammals, including whales.

While the dig was going on, a three-mile boardwalk was built from a ranger station at Ozette Lake across the meadows and bog to the beach near the buried village. The trip was so popular that another boardwalk, this one 3.3 miles long, was built from Sand Point, three miles south of Cape Alava, back to Ozette Lake, giving visitors a good nine-mile walk. The dig was covered up after the major archaeological work was completed, but the boardwalks are still open to the public.

You can reach Ozette Lake by driving west from US 101 on State 112 to the Hoko-Ozette Road just west of Sekiu. The Ozette Lake Ranger Station has a large parking lot.

For more information:

Superintendent, Olympic National Park, 600 East Park Avenue, Port Angeles, WA 98362. 206-452-4501.

GRAYS HARBOR NATIONAL WILDLIFE REFUGE

Ask any Washington bird-watcher where you can see the most birds at any one time, and chances are he or she will say Bowerman Basin. This tidal basin near the Hoquiam Airport west of town is the favored stop for thousands of birds migrating between the Arctic and Central and South America.

The third week of April is usually the best time to catch the birds on their way north. At times the sky is almost filled with flocks flying in tight, synchronized formations. Bird-watchers have learned to get here before dawn and to watch the tide tables, because high tide pushes the shorebirds closer to shore than normal.

About two dozen species of shorebirds can be found at the refuge at different times of the year. Most abundant are western sandpipers (about 85 percent of the entire population), dunlins, short-billed and long-billed dowitchers, and semipalmated plovers. Many dunlins winter over at the refuge. A few hummingbirds also nest in the bushes. Other species include the peregrine falcon, the northern harrier, the red-tailed hawk, and many wading birds, gulls, and terns.

You can reach the refuge by driving west on State 109 toward the coast. Turn left (south) on Paulson Road toward the airport and follow the signs to the refuge, which is just across the road from the airport.

For more information:

Grays Harbor National Wildlife Refuge, c/o Nisqually National Wildlife Refuge, 100 Brown Farm Road, Olympia, WA 98506. 206-753-9467.

Grays Harbor Chamber of Commerce, 506 Duffy Street, Aberdeen WA 98520. 206-532-1924.

DUNGENESS SPIT NATIONAL WILDLIFE REFUGE–RECREATION AREA

The name of the place sounds like a disgusting habit, but in this context, the term *spit* refers to a long neck of land protruding into a body of water. Dungeness Spit does, indeed, protrude. It is supposedly the longest sandspit – 5.5 miles – in the country and is still growing as the currents of the Strait of Juan de Fuca continue depositing sand on it.

The spit juts out from the Dungeness National Wildlife Refuge about three miles from Sequim and angles northeast out into the strait. A little more than halfway out, Graveyard Spit angles off to the south, while the main spit continues on to a lighthouse at the tip. The light has been there since 1858 and is open Thursday through Monday from 9:00 A.M. to 4:00 P.M.

You can reach the spit by following a trail from the parking lot at the edge of the recreation area. The one-half-mile trail leads through a thick coastal forest of firs, hemlocks, and cedars. After descending to the beach, the trail follows along the sand and gravel spit piled high with driftwood. You'll quickly notice how choppy the waves are on the seaward side, but on the other side, only a few feet away, the protected water may be as flat as a pond.

Children enjoy picking through the driftwood and other flotsam, turning the objects into all kinds of toys. Many places are suitable for picnics, and if you're carrying a stove (campfires are not allowed), you can use the debris to build your own temporary cooking shelter, complete with low tables and seats.

The refuge is home to many birds, including harlequin ducks, teals, mergansers, buffleheads, kingfishers, cormorants, grebes, loons, Pacific brant, scoters, wigeon, bald eagles, gyrfalcons, and peregrine falcons. More rare visitors are snowy owls and tufted puffins. Raccoons, sea otters, and harbor seals are common.

A sea otter dining on shellfish

The spit is in the Olympic rain shadow, an odd place sometimes called a blue hole, because in this one zone the Olympic Mountains catch nearly all the rain as it comes in from the Pacific. Rainfall around Dungeness Spit and the nearby retirement town of Sequim is only about fifteen inches annually, but just twenty miles away, it's fifteen *feet* a year. While hiking on Dungeness Spit, you may see dark clouds all around but blue sky directly overhead. You should, however, be prepared for rain and wind. Also, don't forget to bring your own drinking water.

The spit is open from dawn to dusk, and admission is $2.00 per family, which you insert into a slot at the gate.

For more information:

U.S. Fish and Wildlife Service, 1638 Barr Road S., Port Angeles, WA 98382. 206-457-8451.

Clallam County Parks, County Courthouse, Port Angeles WA 98382. 206-452-7831.

2
The Puget Sound Basin

WOODLAND PARK ZOOLOGICAL GARDENS

If my children want to say I deprived them of something, I would have to plead guilty to not taking them to many zoos while they were young. I've never thought one species should have the right to imprison another simply for one's entertainment. When I was young, one of my sisters took me to see the monkey show at the zoo in St. Louis. The monkeys had their own way of dealing with the situation: They threw feces out into the audience, which was tantamount to shouting "Fire!" I cheered for the monkeys.

Things have changed since then, and zoos, particularly the Woodland Park Zoo in Seattle, have taken it upon themselves to serve a more noble function. The Woodland Park Zoo has become an international model for treating its animals with respect and for its work in saving endangered species.

The zoo's first move toward world-class status was building natural habitats, or at least as close as the zookeepers could get so that the animals wouldn't be confined to cages. One such area is the African Savanna for hippos, monkeys, zebras, gorillas, and other African animals.

Another is the Elephant Forest, which is patterned after a Thai logging camp. Tropical Asia is a haven for orangutans, siamangs, lion-tailed macaques, and gorillas. The Tropical Rain Forest is topped with a glass dome.

Coming soon is the Northern Trail, which will exhibit animals and plants from the Arctic coastal plain and the taiga forest region. It will be home to snow leopards (an endangered species), red pandas, mountain goats, marmots, bharal sheep, Kodiak bears, river otters, bald eagles, snowy owls, and other mammals.

Recently, the Center for Wildlife Conservation was established to study and preserve wildlife. It works on projects around the world, in places such as Madagascar, Indonesia, the People's Republic of China, and Tanzania. It also works on breeding animals that normally do not reproduce in captivity, and it will include an expanded wildlife health facility.

The zoo also features the more mundane Family Farm, a place where children can touch and pet several kinds of domesticated animals, including baby goats and piglets.

Woodland Park Zoological Gardens is in the midst of a major expansion at this writing. When it is completed, even its competitors say few zoos in America will be better.

For more information:

Woodland Park Zoological Gardens, 5500 Phinney Avenue North, Seattle, WA 98103-5897. 206-684-4800.

SKAGIT WILDLIFE AREA

You can't really appreciate why snow geese received their name until you've seen several thousand of them swarming around this wildlife area on the Skagit River delta. When they swing around in tight formation, all five or six thousand of them, then suddenly descend to the wet fields below, they look like an organized blizzard. The Washington Department of Wildlife, which manages the area, has counted up to 27,000 snow geese there at one time.

These geese are more accurately called lesser snow geese. They come to the delta each fall from Wrangell Island ninety miles off the coast of Siberia, then return home in the spring. In addition, up to 300 tundra swans and more than 125,000 ducks use the area. Bald eagles, peregrine falcons, northern harriers, red-tailed hawks, and various songbirds are among the other regular visitors and inhabitants. An occasional black-tailed deer, beavers, and river otters are found in the sloughs and channels of the refuge. People driving through the delta en route to La Conner or Conway commonly see farmers cultivating their

Snow geese have both blue and white phases

fields with hundreds or perhaps thousands of birds following along to snatch the worms and bugs exposed by the farm equipment.

The refuge has several miles of trails and dikes, and some of the dead-end roads are good for bird watching. Maps and other information are available at the area's headquarters. To reach it, take the Conway–La Conner exit off I-5, about fifty miles north of Seattle, and follow the signs to the headquarters.

For more information:

Skagit Wildlife Area, 2214 Wylie Road, Mount Vernon, WA 98273. 206-445-4441.

DECEPTION PASS STATE PARK

When my children were small, Deception Pass State Park was one of our favorite places for a weekend outing. The park is about two hours' drive from downtown Seattle, and we had the option of taking the Mukeltio-Clinton ferry one way and driving the length of Whidbey Island, then driving through the tulip and daffodil fields of the Skagit Valley the other. The children loved the park more than any other place we went for picnics, and we invariably went to the same place: Rosario Beach.

This is one of Washington's most popular parks, and because it is so accessible – State 20 goes right through it – it also is the most heavily visited state park. In spite of more than three million visitors each year, the park is so large that it retains its wild flavor. It covers more than 3,000 acres and keeps growing bit by bit as additional land is added. It has more than 250 campsites, 17 miles of saltwater shoreline, 3 freshwater lakes, and more than 20 miles of established trails.

The park is named for Deception Pass, the narrow saltwater channel that separates Whidbey and Fidalgo islands. The explorer Captain George Vancouver gave the pass this name because he had been deceived, thinking that Whidbey Island was a peninsula until he found the pass.

The water rushes through the gap here, creating whirlpools and eddies that are spectacular when seen from the 182-foot-high bridge or from water level on the small island in the middle of the channel. The bridge is nearly 1,000 feet long and is a popular spot for photographers because you can watch the boats running directly beneath you as they attack the saltwater rapids caused by the tidal flows. In the distance, you can see Mount Baker, and to the north are the San Juan Islands.

One of the most beautiful places in the park is Pass Lake, which is right beside the highway and often is as calm as a pond. Motorboats are not permitted, and the calm water reflects the surrounding mountains.

Rosario Beach is a short distance north of Deception Pass. This part of the park is actually a peninsula protruding out into the sound. The peninsula is connected to the mainland by a double beach composed of small, colorful rocks. The northern side is characterized by tidal pools, and the southern side has a boat dock. The peninsula itself is steep and rocky, with little nooks and crannies suitable for spreading out a blanket for a picnic. A trail follows the bay south of the peninsula, with little spurs leading out onto the rocks over the water.

For more information:

Deception Pass State Park, 206-675-2417.

PADILLA BAY NATIONAL ESTUARINE RESEARCH RESERVE

Like so many areas favored by wildlife, Padilla Bay doesn't look especially inviting to the average person who associates saltwater shores with sandy beaches and slowly roasting bodies. When someone like that drives by Padilla Bay's broad mud flats, with views across to the smoking refineries near Anacortes, he or she will keep going until something better comes along. A naturalist, however, whether professional or amateur, will stop, go for a walk, get all muddy and sweaty, and have a wonderful time.

The Padilla Reserve is part of the great Skagit and Stillaguamish deltas, which provide food and cover for millions of waterfowl. This is the place where snow geese and lesser snow geese come to winter over. In fact, more than half of all the lesser snow geese on the Pacific Coast winter here.

Padilla Bay has considerably more to offer than just geese. The reserve encompasses 2,600 acres of eelgrass meadows, marshes, and man-made dikes. The Breazeale–Padilla Bay Interpretative Center sits on a hill overlooking the bay. A mile-long upland trail begins at the center. The reserve also features a short trail down to the beach and a 2.25-mile trail along a dike that was built around the turn of the century when farmers were reclaiming the land from the sea.

Among the wildlife you can expect to see, in addition to the geese during the winter months, are canvasbacks, harlequin ducks, black brant, great blue herons, dunlins, black-bellied plovers, peregrine falcons, and bald eagles. The center has an observation deck and a viewing blind that is open from November through March, and it offers exhibits, classrooms, indoor aquariums, a theater, and a "hands-on" room where you can touch and look at inhabitants of the area.

The center is open from 10:00 A.M. to 5:00 P.M. Wednesday through Sunday. To reach it, drive west from I-5 on State 20 to the Bayview–Edison Road. Turn left (north) onto the road and follow it about five miles to the center.

For more information:

Washington Department of Ecology, 1043 Bayview–Edison Rd., Mount Vernon, WA 98273. 206-428-1558.

SKAGIT VALLEY BULB FARMS

Every year, from April through May and sometimes into June, the Skagit Valley is a mass of color and slow-moving people. This is when tulips, daffodils, irises, and gladiolus bloom. More than 2,000 acres of rich farmland in Washington is given over to flower-bulb growing, and most of it, some 80 percent, is in the Skagit River delta, from I-5 at Mount Vernon and Burlington south and west to Conway and La Conner. All told, Washington grows more bulbs than any other state.

The Skagit Valley farmers got into this business as competition for farmers in the Netherlands (some whisper darkly of selling bulbs to growers over there) because the soil and climate in the Skagit Delta are conducive to growing high-quality bulbs. However, so many people traveling through wanted to buy fresh-cut flowers that the farmers soon opened roadside stands. In most cases, farmers now make more money on cut tulips and daffodils than on bulbs. Iris growers are the only ones who earn more on bulbs than flowers. Farmers in the area also have done well growing grass seed and seed potatoes.

The multicolored fields are a favorite with bicycle riders, families with small children, volksport clubs, and anyone with a love of beautiful flowers. The Mount Vernon Chamber of Commerce sponsors a Tulip Festival each year, including a marathon along the farm roads, and provides a map of the farms open to the public. It is a good time to visit wildlife areas in the vicinity, such as the Skagit Wildlife Area, where the snow geese winter, or Padilla Bay, just north of the bulb farms.

For more information:

Mount Vernon Chamber of Commerce, 325 East College Way, Mount Vernon, WA 98273. 800-428-8547 (42-TULIP).

NORTHWEST TREK WILDLIFE PARK

Northwest Trek, near Eatonville, is one of the more unusual zoos in the state – something on the order of the San Diego Zoo, in that the animals have a lot of room to move around freely and visitors are confined to trams. Northwest Trek opened in 1975 on more than 600 acres of woods and meadows. The property includes several lakes, where you may see migratory birds such as bald eagles, which hunt for fish there.

The zoo's animals include bison, elk, moose, mountain goats, deer, lynx, bobcats, mountain lions, river otters, raccoons, beavers, and several other species. The Cheney Discovery Center has reptiles and amphibians, beehives, and a large fish tank.

The guided tram tour through the zoo takes fifty minutes. Walkers also may follow the five miles of nature trails. A three-quarter-mile loop trail is paved for wheelchairs and strollers. A gift shop and restaurant also are located on the property.

The park is open daily from March through October and Friday through Sunday and some holidays during the rest of the year. Closing time varies with the season.

For more information:

Northwest Trek Wildlife Park, 11610 Trek Drive East, Eatonville, WA 98328. 206-847-1901.

NISQUALLY NATIONAL WILDLIFE RESERVE COMPLEX

In the late 1960s, I worked on the *Seattle Times's Sunday Pictorial* magazine. I was assigned a story about the state's photogrammetry department, which made maps by taking photographs from a plane that flew so slowly it sometimes seemed to hover. The plane took me out over the Nisqually River estuary and spent several minutes going back and forth across it to show me how the photos were taken.

I had never seen a more beautiful place. The delta was broad and flat, and incredibly green. Ribbons of the river meandered in graceful curves on their way to Puget Sound. It was early morning and low tide, so we could see the distinct patterns on the mud flats. I asked our photographer to take some pictures of the delta when we went up in the plane, and the story we published based on his photos received a lot of attention, including some calls and letters from environmental activists who were already working to save the Nisqually Delta from development.

Before long, environmentalists suggested that the entire Nisqually River be made into a park. The river begins on Mount Rainier's Nisqually Glacier, and it is so short that you can see the whole thing from a small plane. You can stand at the glacier and see where the river ends in Puget Sound, and you can stand on the hill overlooking the delta and see Mount Rainier.

The area has historical importance because it was the site of a Hudson's Bay trading post. At McAllister Creek, formerly named Medicine Creek, a treaty between several Native American tribes and Territorial Governor Isaac I. Stevens was signed in 1855 beneath a lone Douglas fir tree that stood beside the creek. That treaty led to prolonged disputes over fishing rights, and several celebrities came to the

A kingfisher on the lookout for fish

area to support the local tribes. Unfortunately, the Treaty Tree was damaged by the construction of I-5 and eventually removed.

As with nearly every effort to protect land from development, the fight to save the Nisqually was long and bitter, and the plan to preserve the entire river didn't get far. But 2,817 acres of the delta were saved. This area is called the Nisqually National Wildlife Refuge and the Nisqually Wildlife Recreation Area. It is one of the largest undisturbed deltas in the state.

The complex is bordered on the north by the Nisqually River and on the south by I-5 and McAllister Creek. A small plot of land also is located on the south side of the creek.

The delta is an excellent place to canoe or kayak because it has many sloughs and branches of the river and creek, and the tall saltwater marsh grass is excellent cover for wildlife. During the spring and summer, the area comes alive with nesting songbirds, swallows, quail, killdeers, mallards, teals, great blue herons, belted kingfishers, and pied-billed grebes. In the fall and spring, migratory birds pass through. Among these are gulls, terns, sandpipers, and ducks. Some, such as wigeon, pintails, and mallards, winter over here.

The complex has photo blinds, an observation deck, seven miles of walking trails, and an interpretive trail with exhibits. It sponsors environmental education activities for school groups and the general public in the Twin Barns Education Center. An admission is charged.

The refuge also is headquarters for the Copalis, Flattery Rocks, and Quillayute Needles national wildlife recreation areas. These islands along the Pacific coast are closed to the public to protect seabird nesting sites.

For more information:

Nisqually National Wildlife Reserve Complex, 100 Brown Farm Road, Olympia, WA 98506. 206-753-9467.

SAN JUAN ISLANDS NATIONAL WILDLIFE REFUGE

All of the San Juan Islands are well within view of Washington's mainland, but whenever I get on a Washington State Ferry or a boat headed for the islands, I usually feel as if I'm embarking on a long voyage. I have traveled with islanders on the ferry, and even after many years of living on the islands, they spend as much of the ride leaning over the rail as any tourist.

Although many of the islands have been thoroughly settled, others remain free of development. Part of the reason for this is the energetic efforts of many citizens and government agencies to declare the islands parks, reserves, and wildlife refuges. Gradually, more bits and pieces are being added to the protected list. One of the largest groups of islands under government protection is the eighty-three islands in the San Juan Islands National Wildlife Refuge. In spite of this seemingly large number, they encompass only 454 acres.

You can visit only two of these islands, Matia and Turn. The others are off-limits. Matia is off the northern end of Orcas Island and a short distance east of Sucia Island State Park. It covers 145 acres and has the 5-acre Marine State Park and a nature trail that's about a mile long. The campsites are in coves along the west side of the island.

Turn Island is just off the tip of San Juan Island and has moorage buoys for boats, which is the only way to reach the thirty-five-acre island. It remains completely wild, with no trails cut through the thick timber.

All the refuge islands are used by glaucous-winged gulls, cormorants, pigeon guillemots, tufted puffins, rhinoceros auklets, black oystercatchers, and numerous shorebirds. Bald eagles use some of them for nesting, and harbor seals occasionally sun themselves on them. A pod of orcas also lives in the San Juans. Except for on Matia and Turn, visitors should stay more than 200 yards away from the islands to avoid frightening nesting birds.

For more information:

San Juan Islands National Wildlife Refuge, c/o Nisqually National Wildlife Reserve Complex, 100 Brown Farm Road, Olympia, WA 98506. 206-753-9467.

GOG-LE-HI-TE WETLAND

With all the recent concern over the disappearance of wetlands, it is worth noting that at least one wetland has been added to the total rather than subtracted. Gog-Le-Hi-Te was built on the Puyallup River near Commencement Bay by the Port of Tacoma to replace a wetland that had been filled in during construction of a container terminal. The project began in 1985; one year and $2.8 million later, it was done.

The name, selected by the Puyallup Indian Tribal Council, means "where land and waters meet." The wetland covers 9.5 acres and comprises mud, marsh, and land. It is home to many varieties of fish and birds. More than 2,000 truckloads of sand, silt, and debris were taken out of the area, and a section of levee was removed to create a mouth to the estuary. A new levee was built around the wetland.

University of Washington scientists created narrow channels, visible now at low tide, throughout the wetland to provide a habitat for small plants and animals. More than

48,000 individual plants of a special marsh grass preferred by wildlife were planted.

The wetland is just off Lincoln Avenue in Tacoma, adjacent to the Puyallup River. It has parking areas, two viewing platforms, and interpretive material.

For more information:

Port of Tacoma, P.O. Box 1837, Tacoma, WA, 98401. 206-383-5841.

WOLF HAVEN

This refuge near Tenino is one of the most unusual in Washington, if not in the entire United States. Wolf Haven is exactly what it says it is: a place for wolves to live free from harm. The founders created the thirty-acre wooded haven when they became aware of the number of wolves that were being mistreated for a variety of reasons. Some were being used in research and then abandoned. Others had been taken in as pets while pups but abandoned when they reached maturity. One was found trotting down a street in Portland, Oregon. The plan was to give the animals a life of dignity and the public a chance to see them.

Among the forty-odd residents, most of which are gray wolves, are representatives of six subspecies, including buffalo wolves, white tundra wolves, and timber wolves. Each animal has its own distinct personality. Some are painfully shy, and others are gregarious to a fault. Some are too dignified to play, whereas others want to do almost nothing else. The staff has neutered some of the animals, but others, especially those from endangered or threatened subspecies, are encouraged to breed.

Visitors are welcome from May through September,

Join in a wolf serenade

from 10:00 A.M. to 5:00 P.M. daily. An admission is charged. Howl-ins are held Friday and Saturday nights when visitors gather around a campfire with the staff for a marshmallow roast, folk music, and discussions about the wolves. Later in the evening, they are encouraged literally to howl with the wolves, and soon the forest is filled with the sound.

The staff has developed an adopt-a-wolf program to

raise funds for food, medical care, and other expenses. Those who join get a certificate, a photo of the wolf, and free visitation rights.

For more information:

Wolf Haven, 3111 Offut Lake Road, Tenino, WA 98589. 206-264-4695.

POINT DEFIANCE ZOO AND AQUARIUM

Also known as the Pacific Rim Zoo, this Tacoma institution focuses its collection on animals from the volcanic countries (the Ring of Fire) around the Pacific Rim. This means that it can have penguins from Antarctica, llamas from South America, Asian elephants, and polar bears. Most zoo rating systems place it among the top five zoos in the country.

The zoo and aquarium are on the same property, which gives visitors a more complete understanding of life around the Pacific and of the interdependence of land and sea animals. The World of Adaptation exhibit has a collection of thirty small mammals, birds, and reptiles from several parts of the world, including Bali mynahs, golden lion tamarins, and black lemurs. The Farm is popular with children because they can get close enough to pet goats, sheep, cows, rabbits, and llamas. The Southeast Asia complex has monkeys, apes, and African and Asian elephants. Penguin Point has a group of the burrowing Magellanic penguins, and Rocky Shores replicates an area near Cape Flattery with walrus, beluga whales, sea otters, seals, sea lions, and puffins. The latter has both above-water and underwater viewing.

The aquarium has an innovative shark display, a

hands-on learning lab, and a South Pacific lagoon. It is home to seals, sea lions, harbor seals, walrus, sea otters, and many other species.

The zoo and aquarium are on Point Defiance, near the Tacoma Narrows Bridge at 5400 North Pearl Street. An admission is charged. They are open daily except Thanksgiving and Christmas.

For more information:

Point Defiance Zoo and Aquarium, 5400 North Pearl Street, Tacoma, WA 98407-5337. 206-591-5335.

3
The Cascade Range—North

NORTH CASCADES NATIONAL PARK

Although the Olympic Peninsula is often called America's Last Wilderness, US 101 had gone all the way around it many years before the North Cascades Highway (State 20) was completed in 1972. Before that time, the road ended on the western approach at Diablo Dam and on the eastern approach at Mazama. Even though this highway goes all the way across the state now, the stretch between Newhalem and Mazama is closed each winter by heavy snowfall, usually from around Christmas until April or May.

The completion of the highway roughly coincided with the creation of North Cascades National Park. The 505,000-acre park was established in 1968 and is one of three major wilderness and recreation areas that are connected: North Cascades National Park, Ross Lake National Recreation Area, and Lake Chelan National Recreation Area.

The park contains some of the most spectacular scenery in America, including jagged peaks that soar almost straight up, high alpine meadows, and hundreds of waterfalls. Its 318 glaciers account for more than half of those in the lower 48 states.

The park has virtually no roads but thousands of miles of trails. Most of these depart from the North Cascades Highway, but others are accessible only by taking a boat or plane to Stehekin, at the northern tip of Lake Chelan, and then entering the wilderness there.

Ross Lake National Recreation Area forms a corridor through the park, dividing it into two sections. Most of this area is along the North Cascades Highway and encompasses 107,000 acres. Included in the recreation area are Seattle City Light's Diablo Lake and Ross Dam tours. Food, lodging, boat rentals, tackle, licenses, and camping supplies are available.

Lake Chelan National Recreation Area begins about halfway up the lake and continues on into the North Cascades to include the town of Stehekin, some ranches and private residences, and the trail from Stehekin to Cascade Pass. Lake Chelan is 1,500 feet deep in one place, making it one of the nation's deepest lakes.

The most popular part of this recreation area is Stehekin, about fifty miles up the lake. This town has survived up in the mountains for most of this century. It is the most isolated town in Washington because it has never had a road into it and is fifty miles by water from Chelan. You must either take the daily boat in from Chelan or fly in on the small airline that operates float planes. Shuttle buses run from Stehekin up the valley to the national park entrance, and several concessionaires offer food, lodging, and outdoor activities, including river rafting, horseback riding, nature walks, and boat rentals.

The national park is further protected by the Pasayten Wilderness on the northeast border. Its northern boundary is the international border with Canada. Manning Provincial Park shares part of this boundary with the national park.

Early in the campaign for national park status, opponents of pure wilderness wanted to build aerial tramways into various parts of the North Cascades. One argument was that this would allow those who are physically challenged to enjoy the wilderness. No tramways or other mechanical intrusions were permitted, but the mile-long Rainy Pass Recreation Trail, leading into a beautiful subalpine area, is accessible to visitors in wheelchairs.

On the whole, the park remains reasonably inaccessible. The long winters with the highway closed, the lack of many other roads, the rugged terrain, and the long distances from one highway point to another ensure this inaccessibility. By far the most popular way to enjoy the park is by driving through it on the spectacular North Cascades Highway, stopping at the few small towns and scenic turnouts, and going for short walks into the forest or along the streams and lakes.

For more information:

North Cascades National Park, 800 State Street, Sedro Woolley, WA 98284. 206-856-5700.

ESMERALDA BASIN

If you want to hike into a beautiful area, set up camp, and then go on day hikes from there, Esmeralda Basin is the place for you. Many years ago, my family found it almost perfect for our needs. The only problem we encountered was finding a place to camp away from the trudging hordes on their way over one of the passes. We eventually solved the problem when we found a spot in the woods away from the trail.

Esmeralda Basin is back in the mountains north of Cle Elum, reached by driving north on US 97, turning left (west) on North Fork Teanaway River Road, and following it twenty-three miles to the trailhead. The route follows an old mining road for about two miles, then the basin opens up, with mountains all around.

Three routes lead out of the basin and over the mountains. Fortune Creek Pass is to the west, Ingalls Pass goes straight ahead to the north, and Long's Pass is to the east. Each pass is worth a day hike from base camp in the basin. We hiked most of the way to Fortune Creek Pass, going past old mining shacks and getting the scare of our lives when an enormous sheet of ice broke free of the sheer face of a mountain and landed nearby with a boom.

The next day we hiked to the summit of Ingalls Pass and were treated to a rain shower that briefly became a snow shower while we were eating our freeze-dried lunch. Our hike was early in the summer, and some snow was still visible along the trails. Enough had cleared, though, for us to enjoy the masses of wildflowers that follow close behind as the snow line moves uphill.

A word of warning is in order here. We made the hike several years ago, when nearly everyone who walked more than 100 yards from the trailheads was there for enjoyment rather than mischief. We thought nothing of abandoning our tents and most of our gear for hours at a time. Things have changed in the Northwest. The population has increased, as has the crime rate. Thus, you probably should not leave anything behind if you choose to go on day hikes out of this or any other basin.

For more information:

Wenatchee National Forest, 301 Yakima Street, Wenatchee, WA 98807-0811. 509-662-4335.

HARTS PASS AND SLATE PEAK

It isn't often that you'll have a chance to look down onto the Pacific Crest Trail, but if you drive to the summit of Slate Peak, you can do just that. At 7,440 feet, Slate Peak is the highest point in Washington to which you can take the family car.

To reach the peak, turn off State 20 (North Cascades Highway) at Mazama and drive eighteen miles along the narrow switchback that leads steadily up into the North Cascades. At the first turnout, you'll have a sweeping view of the Methow Valley and Goat Wall below. Other impressive views open up at virtually every turn, but unfortunately, you'll find very few places to stop for a look or photographs.

A large parking lot is located at the 6,797-foot summit of Harts Pass, where the Pacific Crest Trail comes through. You can stop here for a hike along the trail. No matter which direction you go, you'll soon find great views of the Cascade Range and the mountains of North Cascades National Park.

The road forks at the pass. The left, or south, fork leads down to remnants of two old mining towns, Barron and Chancellor. Barron is on private land behind a locked gate; Chancellor is farther along on a rough road.

The other alternative is to continue on the main road to the right and follow it to its end at a gate just below the summit of Slate Peak. The top of the peak was scraped off to accommodate a U.S. Army radar station, which has been abandoned but is open for shelter. At the summit, you'll have a 360-degree view of the Cascades. Far below to the west, you may see backpackers or horseback riders making their way along the winding Pacific Crest Trail. Displays at the summit identify the surrounding mountains.

You have several options for hiking in the area. It is above the timberline, and trails lead out through meadows and up to the ridge.

If you decide to stay overnight, you have a choice of established campgrounds. (It's best to bring your own water if you plan to camp anywhere in the high country.) Among these are one at the summit of Harts Pass; Meadows, at the 6,300-foot level south of the pass; and River Bend and Ballard, both at lower elevations.

For more information:

Early Winters Forest Service Information Center, Winthrop, WA 98862. 509-996-2266.

PACIFIC CREST TRAIL

This is the mother of all West Coast trails, and I doubt that you'll find anyone who has ever hiked who hasn't wanted to hike at least a portion of its 2,620-mile length from Canada to Mexico. One of my many dreams is to hike the portion described here, from Stevens Pass to Snoqualmie Pass.

The trail's name is a bit misleading because although it stays in the high country most of the time, it doesn't stick strictly to the crests of the Cascades and Sierras. It is a tough trip, and most people take two or three summers to complete it. Hiking it is a logistical nightmare because you must have food and equipment mailed ahead to places where the trail crosses highways or other roads, and you are out of touch with civilization for several days at a time. I suspect, however, that with cellular phones becoming so popular, more and more hikers will make this trek while talking to the folks back home.

In the Northwest, this trail is often called the Cascade

Crest Trail because that was its original name before the whole route was declared a National Scenic Trail in 1968 and given the formal name of the Pacific Crest National Scenic Trail. Some of it was rerouted to higher elevations to bypass environmentally sensitive areas and lowlands and to more accurately reflect its name. Most of it now lies in U.S. Forest Service and national park land.

I selected the Sevens Pass–to–Snoqualmie Pass segment because of ease of transportation. Commercial bus service is available at each pass, and it is a short drive for someone picking up the hiker. The hike described here is about seventy miles long. I would allow a week for it, but younger hikers or speed hikers might be able to do it in a couple of days less.

In this segment, the trail's elevation ranges from about 3,000 feet to more than 6,000 feet, and much of it is quite steep. However, this is one of the most beautiful sections of the trail. It crosses many streams, traverses open meadows, goes around lakes, climbs to the tops of ridges and follows them for long distances, and goes through thick, silent forests.

Long before you go, check with the Forest Service and outdoor organizations for the latest information on the trail. The Forest Service sells good maps of the trail and issues occasional bulletins with up-to-date information. These are available from any of the national forests the trail touches. The portion of the trail described here goes through Wenatchee National Forest and Mount Baker–Snoqualmie National Forest.

For more information:

Wenatchee National Forest, 301 Yakima Street, Wenatchee, WA 98807-0811. 509-662-4335.

Mount Baker–Snoqualmie National Forest, 21905

Sixty-fourth Avenue West, Mountlake Terrace, WA 98043. 206-775-9702.

GIFFORD PINCHOT NATIONAL FOREST

One of the most popular activities in Gifford Pinchot National Forest is picking the huckleberries that grow there in profusion. Families in the area have been doing this for generations, and the Native Americans of the area depended on the berries for at least 10,000 years.

Berries were so important to the Indians that they created religious ceremonies to thank their gods for them and the other wild foods that sustained them. When the territorial governor of Washington Territory went through the region negotiating treaties with all the tribes, those in this

Pick some huckleberries

area insisted that they retain rights to their sources of these foods. The treaty signed by President James Buchanan on June 9, 1855, created the Yakima Reservation. It stipulated that "the exclusive right of taking fish in all the streams, where running through or bordering said reservation, is further secured to said confederated tribes and bands of Indians . . . together with the privilege of hunting, [and] gathering roots and berries."

It would be nearly eighty years before the Native Americans could exercise this exclusive right. Not until 1932 did the federal government set aside a specific area within Gifford Pinchot National Forest exclusively for members of the Yakima tribe. This area is relatively small, but it is well marked. It is located northwest of Trout Lake on the east side of Forest Service Road 24. The Native Americans also have the right to pick berries anywhere else they please. The largest berry patches outside the restricted area are on either side of Forest Service Roads 60, 6020, 65, 30, and 64.

Over the years, a small subculture has grown up around the berries, and people take them very seriously. Discussions and debates concerning how best to maintain the quality of the berry patches are common. There is little doubt that fires are essential to keeping competing plants away from the berries. In pre-Columbia–Basin days, the Native Americans routinely burned the patches after the fall harvest to ensure their future.

The Native Americans spent the summer and early fall in the high country hunting, fishing, and picking berries. They dried some of these berries for use in the winter. When the cold weather came, they moved back down to the Columbia Gorge and their winter villages, where they traded goods, including berries, for things that they needed.

The Forest Service recommends these methods of preserving huckleberries:

Freezing: For desserts, pack in medium syrup. Or pack in sugar, using one cup to eight to nine cups of berries. For pies, dry without sugar or syrup.
Drying: Sort, wash, and leave whole. You can either leave them as they are, steam them for thirty seconds to one minute, or crack them by dipping them for fifteen to thirty seconds in boiling water, then placing them in cold water and removing any excess moisture. Spread the berries in a layer not more than two berries deep. A cloth on the tray may help keep the berries from sticking. Drying takes about four hours in a dehydrator at 135 degrees. Dry until they are hard and rattle when shaken. Crush a berry between your fingers to make sure no moisture remains.

For more information:

Gifford Pinchot National Forest, 6926 East Fourth Plain Boulevard, Vancouver, WA 98668-8944. 206-696-7500.

OAK CREEK WILDLIFE AREA

If you want to see elk, this is the place to go. Although the refuge harbors other animals and birds, the winter feeding program for elk attracts the most attention and visitors.

The refuge was created after development (mostly orchards and subdivisions) replaced much of the elk's winter habitat. As the elk herds grew smaller, the state acquired 84,000 acres of lowlands to accommodate them in the winter. At Oak Creek, Washington Department of Wildlife employees scatter bales of hay throughout the area to feed the elk. At almost any given time during the winter, you can see anywhere from a dozen to several hundred elk calmly dining on the hay.

The refuge also is a good place to see golden eagles,

prairie falcons, various hawks, Lewis's woodpeckers, western tanagers, bluebirds, and other songbirds. The relatively uncommon western gray squirrel lives along Oak Creek, and occasionally you will see California bighorn sheep.

The wildlife area is located just off US 12 West of Naches.

For more information:

Oak Creek Wildlife Area, 16601 Highway 12, Naches, WA 98937. 509-653-2390.

COLUMBIA RIVER GORGE NATIONAL SCENIC AREA

Hardly a month goes by without newspapers carrying a story about the continuing dispute over the creation (in 1986) of this scenic area. Environmentalists love it, but local people, many of whom relied on logging for income, feel that it has had a negative effect on their lives. Much of this controversy has coincided with the loss of additional logging-related jobs due to the spotted owl debate.

The Columbia Gorge is one of western America's genuine treasures. Not only is it an incredibly beautiful area, but it is also geologically, historically, and ecologically unusual. In some ways, particularly regarding plant life, it is unique.

The protected area covers some 292,000 acres on both sides of the river, running upstream (east) from the city limits of Vancouver to Maryhill Museum near where US 97 crosses the river. Thus, it goes from the flatland where the Lower Columbia floodplain begins and continues entirely through the Cascade Range to the basaltic buttes of central and eastern Washington.

The scenic area was created to prevent the gorge from being exposed to clear-cutting and industrial and residential development. To keep a measure of local control, the scenic designation created a partnership between the Forest Service, the Columbia River Gorge Commission, several Native American tribal governments, and the six counties affected. In addition, the Oregon and Washington state governments were involved.

A leisurely drive up the gorge will give you an idea of why it has been saved and why opponents were so concerned about losing control of the forests surrounding it. The Oregon side of the gorge has the most sheer topography, and consequently the most waterfalls. The Washington side has the most severely eroded mountains, many of which have crumbled and fallen into the river in the slow march of geologic history. Oregon has the fastest route, I-84, through the area, but the Washington route (State 14) is less heavily traveled and thus more leisurely.

State 14 begins in Vancouver and follows the river faithfully, side by side with the tracks for the Burlington Northern railroad. Below Bonneville Dam, the river is broad and slow as it flows freely on its way to the sea. Its banks are lined with dikes, which it still overflows from time to time.

The first dramatic viewpoint is at Cape Horn, just below Bonneville Dam, where the road goes around an enormous rock that offers views of the river in both directions. It passes the famed Beacon Rock, which some say is the second largest monolith in the world behind Gibraltar. I can't verify this fact, but I can tell you that the rock is very imposing. It was saved from being turned into a quarry many years ago and is now a state park.

One of the most interesting geological aspects of the gorge is the effect the great floods of the ice ages had on it.

(For more on this, see the section on the Channeled Scablands in Chapter 6.) These floods occurred when glaciers blocked the Clark Fork River east of Lake Pend Oreille in northern Idaho and formed ice dams up to 2,000 feet high. This created lakes covering up to 3,000 square miles and containing about half as much water as Lake Michigan. When these ice dams burst, the water came roaring across the Columbia Plateau in a flow more than sixty times the volume of the Amazon River, creating a vast landscape of dry coulees, falls, and channels.

When the water hit the Wallula Gap south of Pasco, the flood crest was at 1,200 feet. The Columbia River Gorge turned the flood downriver, and the rushing water stripped vegetation off the gorge walls. The flood carried big chunks of ice with granite and schist boulders in them. Many of these rocks, called erratics, have been found along the gorge. One was found at the 970-foot elevation some 10 miles back in the mountains.

The scenic area is home to a wide variety of plants, nine that are unique to the area and fifty-eight others that are candidates for threatened and endangered species lists. One of the greatest concentrations of rare plants is in the area between the White Salmon and Klickitat rivers, also an area where the wet, moderate coastal climate meets the dry, extreme climate of eastern Washington.

Five species of animals here are on the U.S. Fish and Wildlife Service's candidate list: the western spotted frog, northern spotted owl, northern bald eagle, Arctic peregrine falcon, and Aleutian Canada goose. The Columbia white-tailed deer was present in the gorge at one time, but it is protected on its own refuge on the Lower Columbia. (See the section on the Julia Butler Hansen National Wildlife Refuge in Chapter 4.)

You will have plenty of opportunities to stop and enjoy

the view, visit a winery, or spend the night in either a new or older resort. Federal and local government agencies run numerous campgrounds throughout the scenic area.

The scenic area ends just before you reach US 97, one of the major north-south routes through central Washington and Oregon.

For more information:

Columbia River Gorge National Scenic Area, 902 Wasco Avenue, Suite 200, Hood River, OR 97031. 503-386-2333.

Washington State Parks Information, 7150 Cleanwater Lane, K4-11, Olympia, WA 98504-5711. 206-753-5755.

Gifford Pinchot National Forest, 6926 East Fourth Plain Boulevard, Vancouver, WA 98668-8944. 206-750-5000.

Camas-Washougal Chamber of Commerce, 422 N.E. Fourth Avenue, Camas, WA 98607. 206-834-2472.

Skamania County Chamber of Commerce, P.O. Box 1037, Stevenson, WA 98648. 509-427-8911.

Mount Adams Chamber of Commerce, P.O. Box 449, White Salmon, WA 98672. 509-493-3630.

Klickitat County Tourism Committee, P.O. Box 1220, Goldendale, WA 98620. 509-773-3466.

4 Southwest Washington

WILLAPA NATIONAL WILDLIFE REFUGE

Willapa Bay, one of the few major estuaries on the West Coast that is still reasonably intact, is one of Washington's natural treasures. It is the largest oyster-producing area on the West Coast and one of the major wintering, resting, and feeding areas along the Pacific flyway. As a result, more than 20,000 acres of the estuary have been set aside as a wildlife refuge.

The bay is the estuary for several rivers and streams, among them the Naselle, Bear, and Palix rivers, as well as the North, Middle, and South forks of the Nemah River. Most of the bay is protected by the Long Beach Peninsula, and much of it is shallow and muddy at low tide, with the winding freshwater streams running like arteries through the soft mud.

The centerpiece of the refuge is Long Island, but the refuge also includes a large saltwater marsh at the mouth of the Bear River, and the Reikkola Unit near Long Beach has diked grasslands managed for migratory waterfowl. Leadbetter Point, a sandy peninsula that protrudes from the northern tip of the Long Beach Peninsula, is another area of interest.

A kayaker at Willapa

Long Island is perhaps the best-known portion of the refuge because it is the most isolated and has 274-acre Cedar Grove, one of the last such groves in the state. You must use your own boat to travel to the island. The ferry that serves it is owned by a logging company and is not allowed to transport visitors to the refuge. This means that if you decide to visit the island, you must have a refuge map and a local tide table. You'll need the map to find one of the few places where you can land your boat. None of them is an improved site, and some landings can be used only at high tide. When you tie up the boat, make sure it will still be there after the tide goes out.

Cedar Grove is reached by hiking along the Trail of Ancient Cedars, which is about three-quarters of a mile from the main road. The trees have been protected from the most damaging storms by local geography and their own particular shapes, and the island setting protects them from fires. In the past, other similar groves were logged, but this grove was saved because it was difficult to enter with logging equipment.

The climate is mild and wet, so the floor of the Long Island forest is covered with lush vegetation: salal, huckleberry, salmonberry, and various other low-growing plants. Trees include western hemlock, Sitka spruce, and western red cedar.

Numerous birds live here, including bald eagles, olive-sided flycatchers, western flycatchers, western wood pewees, ravens, golden-crowned kinglets, Townsend's warblers, yellow-rumped warblers, Steller's jays, varied thrushes, solitary vireos, western tanagers, dark-eyed juncos, purple finches, pine siskins, northern saw-whet owls, barred owls, Vaux's swifts, pileated woodpeckers, tree swallows, chestnut-backed chickadees, and red-breasted nuthatches. Mammals include Douglas squirrels, northern flying squirrels, raccoons, Townsend's chipmunks, southern red-backed voles, deer, black bears, and elk. Bow hunting only is permitted.

Leadbetter Point was added to the refuge because of its open water, sand dunes, and pine forest, which make it very attractive to migratory waterfowl. Its residents include thousands of black brant, which come here to feed and rest on their migrations between Alaska and Mexico. Red knots, pectoral sandpipers, snowy plovers (sections of the beach are closed from April through August to protect the plovers' nests), brown pelicans, and trumpeter and tundra swans also are visitors.

Refuge headquarters are on US 101 near the mouth of the Naselle River. Here you can get information on the refuge and directions for going to Long Island. Leadbetter Point is about fifteen miles north of the town of Long Beach on State 1030.

For more information:

Willapa National Wildlife Refuge, HC 01 Box 910, Ilwaco, WA 98624. 206-484-3482.

JULIA BUTLER HANSEN NATIONAL WILDLIFE REFUGE

Originally named for the subspecies it was established to protect, the Columbia white-tailed deer, this important refuge on the Lower Columbia River was renamed in 1988 to honor the late Washington state legislator and U.S. representative. The refuge was created in 1972 to protect the subspecies that at one time biologists thought was extinct. This smaller relative of the white-tailed deer was once common from the Umpqua River in Oregon north into the

Puget Sound basin. It was first described by Lewis and Clark, who said that it was abundant from The Dalles to the river estuary.

Although the species was believed to be extinct by the 1930s, about 230 stragglers were found in the area where the refuge was established. A few more were found along the Umpqua River in Oregon. The Columbia River herd has grown to around 900, and the U.S. Fish and Wildlife Service foresees a time when the species can be reclassified as threatened or even removed entirely from the endangered species list.

The 4,000-acre refuge is in two pieces. The main portion lies between State 4 and the Columbia River, beginning about two miles west of Cathlamet. The Elochoman River forms its eastern boundary. This portion goes all the way north to the small, picturesque town of Skamokawa. The second portion is Tenasillahe Island in the middle of the Columbia.

Some farming is permitted in the refuge, and the open fields are used for livestock grazing and haying, which create green forage for the deer. Along the highway, you may see a herd of cows and a few deer grazing side by side. Some crops are grown to control weeds and for additional wildlife food. Some of the open fields have been permitted to return to their natural state to provide more cover.

One unwelcome refuge visitor is the Roosevelt elk. These animals trample the underbrush and prevent deer from using the cover. When the elk population becomes too large, they are removed from the area.

A number of birds visit the refuge, including swans, Canada geese, ducks, bald eagles, red-tailed hawks, black-shouldered kites, blue herons, grebes, loons, cormorants, snipes, and various songbirds. Snipes are famous for their courtship flight, during which a rapid dive display produces

Columbia white-tailed deer

an eerie wailing sound as the wind whistles through the bird's vibrating tail feathers. This sound may be mistaken for an owl's call and is known as winnowing.

The refuge is an easy place to watch wildlife because it is surrounded by good roads. A dike road follows the riverbank, and Brooks Road goes along Brooks Slough on the western side. You can also walk along Center Road, which leads from the refuge headquarters at the Elochoman River to the dike road along Steamboat Slough. Hunting is permitted, but only for migratory birds.

For more information:

Refuge Manager, Julia Butler Hansen National Wildlife Refuge, P.O. Box 566, Cathlamet, WA 98612. 206-795-3915.

RIDGEFIELD NATIONAL WILDLIFE REFUGE

So many of Washington's national wildlife refuges are in open, sometimes barren country that it is a treat to find one that has meadows, streams, trees, farms, marshes, ponds, and a lot of wildlife. This refuge, located about twenty miles north of Vancouver on the Columbia River, has all those things and more.

The 4,627-acre refuge is entirely open (many refuges have closed nesting areas), and the only time visitors are restricted to certain areas is for safety during hunting season. It borders the pretty town of Ridgefield on three sides and covers most of the Lewis River where it enters the Columbia. The refuge includes several lakes, including Rest and Campbell, and numerous sloughs, seasonal marshes, and small streams.

This refuge has two parts. The northern part is called the Carty Unit and is accessible from Main Street in Ridgefield. Just inside the unit is the Oak Grove Nature Trail, which meanders among the oak trees, bogs, and open pastures. The southern unit is called River S. Its entrance is on South Ninth Street, and it has several miles of good gravel roads, where you can watch wildlife from your car.

Ridgefield National Wildlife Refuge is an important resting and wintering place for dusky and other subspecies of Canada geese, tundra swans, and ducks. Sandhill cranes visit during the fall and spring, and a wide variety of songbirds, water birds, shorebirds, and raptors also inhabit the area.

Small mammals live in the refuge. Among these is the unwanted nutria, which is sometimes mistaken for a muskrat. This rodent was brought here from South America by would-be fur farmers, but individual animals escaped, and it has become a major pest in some areas.

The refuge has a full schedule of wildlife study and observation, as well as environmental educational aids for teachers. Some fishing and waterfowl hunting is permitted in season.

To reach the refuge, take I-5 to Ridgefield (exit 14). Drive three miles west to town. Follow the signs to the refuge entrances.

For more information:

Ridgefield National Wildlife Refuge, 301 North Third Street, Ridgefield, WA 98642. 206-887-4106.

5 The Cascade Range—South

MOUNT RAINIER NATIONAL PARK

You won't be in the Puget Sound basin long before you'll hear someone say, Boy, the mountain is really out today. Once you've seen Mount Rainier looming on the southeast horizon in the morning light, you'll understand why locals refer to it simply as the mountain. Its appearance changes from day to day, hour to hour, and sometimes, especially during the winter months, it won't be visible for weeks on end because of overcast skies.

Mount Rainier stands 14,410 feet above sea level, and this elevation is exaggerated somewhat by the low mountains of the Cascade Range surrounding it. It has the most glaciers of any American mountain outside Alaska. The mountain is encircled by the Wonderland Trail, which is 93 miles long. The park itself covers 235,612 acres. It was established in 1899 as the United States' fifth national park.

Mount Rainier's volcano has not erupted for several thousand years, but sulfuric steam still vents around the summit, and volcanologists keep an eye on it just in case. It does have a history of heating up and causing catastrophic mud slides, and such an event could create a disaster between the mountain and Puget Sound similar to that caused by the eruption of Mount St. Helens in 1980.

The national park has an excellent highway system that goes part of the way around the mountain. The most ambitious network of roads is along the southern boundary, where the most visitor services are found. This joins a north-south road that has only one major stop, at the Sunrise Visitor Center. Two lesser roads enter from the northwest and dead-end after about ten miles.

Nearly all visitors arrive via the Nisqually Entrance on State 706 from the Tacoma area. The highway leads to Longmire, the former park headquarters, which is now a museum. The National Park Inn has sixteen rooms and a restaurant and is open year-round.

The busiest places in the park are the Henry M. Jackson Memorial Visitor Center, with a grandstand view of the mountain and a restaurant, and Paradise, which has a large inn and other facilities. Farther on, and some distance downhill, is the lush forest at Ohanapecosh, where you can take short hikes through the old-growth forest. On the eastern side of the mountain is Sunrise, a day-use area that has equally stunning views of the mountain.

All these visitor areas have trails leading toward the mountain or back into the forest. Only Longmire remains open year-round. One reason the others close is snow: Paradise gets an average of 620 inches of snow each year, often more.

Those who plan to do the park in one day will be disappointed because the road through it is both extremely beautiful and slow. If you aren't camping and you can't get a room reservation inside the park, it's a good idea to stay nearby so that you can really enjoy the scenery. Whether you are simply a drive-through visitor or a hiker-camper, make plans well in advance.

Hundreds of people climb to the summit each year, but it's not an easy climb. Many climbers have been killed by avalanches, falling rocks, hypothermia, and falling into crevasses. All climbers must register with the park service before setting out, and the park service strongly urges climbers to go join an expedition led by the long-established concessionaire Rainier Mountaineering, Inc. A normal climb takes two days: one day to a shelter at about the 10,000-foot mark and the second day to the summit and back down to the base.

The park has information on the 300-plus miles of trails, including the 93-mile Wonderland Trail. The latter goes through the major campgrounds, so it is easy to make the hike in segments rather than taking on the entire route in a single outing.

One of the most popular trails is the Spray Park Trail in the northwest corner. You can reach it by entering at the Mowich Lake entrance from State 165 and driving 16 miles on a rough road to the lake. The Mowich to Spray Park Trail is about 7 miles round-trip and has an elevation gain of about 1,000 feet. Another popular hike is from Mowich Lake to Tolmie Peak, about the same distance and elevation

Mountain goat mother and child

gain. Both offer dramatic views of the mountain and lead through pretty open meadows and dense forests.

One of the park's major attractions is the blanket of wildflowers that covers the ground every year. The seasons move up and down the slopes, and a given hike may take you from spring flowers through summer and into fall. The park also attracts a variety of animals. I once saw a large deer grazing peacefully a few hundred feet inside the Carbon River Entrance while guns were being fired at his relatives in the distance. Among the wildlife you may see are ground squirrels, chipmunks, marmots, pikas, deer, elk, and black bears. Only occasionally will you see mountain goats. Birds include Steller's jays, gray jays, ravens, and Clark nutcrackers.

A fee of $5.00 per vehicle is charged for each entrance, or a $15.00 annual pass is available. Check with the National Park Service concerning the Golden Eagle Passport for senior citizens over the age of sixty-two.

For more information:

Superintendent, Mount Rainier National Park, Ashford, WA 98304. 206-569-2211.

Mowich Lake and Spray Park, Carbon River Ranger Station, 206-569-2211, ext. 2358.

Mount Rainier Guest Services, 55106 Kernahan Road East, Ashford, WA 98304. 206-569-2275.

Rainier Mountaineering, Inc., June-September: Paradise, WA 98398; October-May: 535 Dock Street, Suite 209, Tacoma, WA 98402. 206-627-6242.

INDIAN HEAVEN WILDERNESS AREA

For centuries, this area was a favorite gathering place for Native Americans. One of the most distinctive remnants of this culture is the Indian Race Track, where the tribes gathered for horse races. Ruts made by the horses are still visible, like the wagon ruts along sections of the Oregon Trail.

The Indian Race Track is at the southern tip of the wilderness, a long hike from the major approaches. However, it is only a short distance from the Pacific Crest Trail and not far from the northwestern edge of the Big Lava Flow, a major landmark south of Indian Heaven. Be sure to get a map from the Forest Service, either at Gifford Pinchot National Forest headquarters in Vancouver or the ranger office in Trout Lake.

The Pacific Crest Trail traverses almost the entire wilderness, and many visitors drive to the trail from Trout Lake on Forest Service Road 24, which approaches it on the east and north sides. About forty miles of trail lead through Indian Heaven, and its relatively flat terrain makes it popular with cross-country skiers. The wilderness also has a number of small lakes.

For more information:

Gifford Pinchot National Forest, 6926 East Fourth Plain Boulevard, Vancouver, WA 98668-8944. 206-750-5000.

Mount Adams Ranger District, Trout Lake, WA 98650. 509-295-2501.

MOUNTAIN LOOP HIGHWAY

This popular sixty-mile loop drive is generally thought of as a pleasant way to spend a long summer day, as it traverses some of the prettiest country you'll find on the western slope of the Cascade Range. It is also a good way to enjoy the wildlife of the Cascades, including fish, fowl, and mammals.

Most people drive the route from the south end at Granite Falls. The first stop is at the Granite Falls Fishway, which for many years was the longest fish ladder in the world. It is an impressive sight. You can stop and park on the west side of the bridge that spans the South Fork Stillaguamish River, which local people refer to simply as the Stilly. The bridge crosses the series of falls, and a good trail leads down the steep grade beside the fish ladder. You may never see a fish through the grill that covers the ladder,

Migrating salmon

but the hike to the foot of the falls is pleasant in all seasons and all kinds of weather.

For the next several miles you follow the crooked course of the Stilly, and you'll undoubtedly see dozens of fishermen working the pools and riffles for eastern brook trout, rainbow trout, sea-run cutthroat trout, steelhead, and, of course, salmon. From October through February, you can see migrating coho salmon working their way upstream to the shallow Gold Basin Pond near the tiny town of Verlot. You also may see bald eagles here for the annual feast.

A little farther upstream is the Big Four Boardwalk, which leads out to the beaver dams where waterfowl and songbirds live. Off in the distance, you may see mountain goats grazing in the high country. Deer and elk also frequent the area.

The road becomes gravel when it turns north to follow the Sauk River into Darrington. Off this river road are several rougher ones leading to trailheads. These trails take you back into Glacier Peak, the Henry M. Jackson Wilderness Area, and several other destinations popular among backpackers. Several Forest Service campgrounds are located along the Sauk River.

From the logging town of Darrington, the loop heads west on State 530 to emerge at Arlington. This road has several turnouts to campgrounds. One of the best is French Creek Campground, which has a trail leading back into the dense forest and past a series of waterfalls. Other roads lead back into the forest to lakes, some natural and others behind beaver ponds.

For more information:

Mount Baker–Snoqualmie National Forest, 21905 Sixty-fourth Avenue West, Mountlake Terrace, WA 98043. 206-775-9702.

Washington Department of Wildlife, 600 Capitol Way North, Olympia, WA 98501-1091. 206-753-5707.

MOUNT ST. HELENS NATIONAL VOLCANIC MONUMENT

Europeans hadn't been in the Northwest long before they saw steam and ash spewing from the summit of a mountain that was almost a perfect cone. Captain George Vancouver named it in honor of a personal friend, Alleyne Fitzherbert, the Baron of St. Helens, England's ambassador to Spain, and the Native Americans in the area referred to it as the mountain that smoked. The 9,677-foot peak was a favorite of almost everyone who saw it, and it was a relatively easy climb from Spirit Lake, where millions of photographs were taken showing the almost perfect cone of the mountain reflected in the lake.

During the late winter and early spring of 1980, the mountain began heating up. Tremors of varying magnitude rippled through it, and steam began venting ominously. New craters were created around the summit, and steam and ash began shooting into the sky. Volcanologists were almost positive a major eruption was on its way, but they had no way of predicting exactly when.

It came on Sunday, May 18, 1980, at 8:32 A.M. The eruption shot from the northeast side of the mountain in a tremendous explosion. The blast blew 1,312 feet off the summit; flattened 60,000 acres (150 square miles) of forest; killed 57 persons; destroyed more than 220 homes, 17 miles of railroad tracks, 4.5 billion board feet of lumber, and an estimated 5,000 deer and 1,500 elk; and sent forth an ash cloud that brought darkness to communities across the state and into Idaho and Montana. The beautiful Spirit Lake disappeared beneath the mud and ash, and the Toutle,

Cowlitz, and Columbia rivers were clogged with debris. Total property damage was assessed at $1.1 billion.

For several years following the blast, most of the area around the mountain was off-limits while the volcano cooled down and the devastated area was made safe. The area was declared a national monument, and gradually more and more roads and trails were built to make the area accessible to visitors.

Mount St. Helens is now one of Washington's most popular attractions, as well as an excellent laboratory for studying not only volcanoes but also how plant and animal life regenerates after such an event. Roads that disappeared in the eruption have been replaced and in some cases relocated so that they will be safer in the event of future mud slides or other volcanic activity. The crater area is still off-limits, but you can hike all the way around the base.

The newest road is State 504 from I-5 at Castle Rock. This route is good for people with only one day to visit the volcano because you can stop at the Mount St. Helens Visitor Center on State 504 five miles from I-5 on your way in. The center has an exhibit with a walk-through model of a volcano that shows how magma (molten rock) flows through a volcano's plumbing system.

The road dead-ends at the newest visitor center on Coldwater Ridge, where you can virtually stare into the volcano's mouth only seven miles away. This center has a number of displays, including some with talking mannequins, with an emphasis on the regeneration of life. The center also has a fast-food restaurant and picnic area.

Another route is south from US 12 at Randle on Forest Service Road 25. Spurs lead off this main route to Bear Meadow, where the most famous photo of the eruption was taken; to Miner's Car, where a car was sandblasted and thrown more than fifty feet by the eruption; to Norway

Pass; and to Harmony Viewpoint, where you can hike a mile to the remains of Spirit Lake. A longer eight-mile hike leads across the desolate Plains of Abraham. The twenty-seven-mile Loowit Trail goes all the way around the mountain.

On the southern flank of the mountain, approached either by continuing the previous route or by taking State 503 from I-5 at Woodland, you can see how the mountainsides looked before the 1980 eruption. The slopes here show the results of earlier eruptions, including Ape Cave, the longest intact lava tube in the continental United States. The cave was formed, apparently about the time of Christ, when a river of lava cooled enough for a crust to form over it. The lava continued to flow beneath the crust until most of it drained away, leaving the cave. The main entrance is roughly at the midpoint of the tube, and the Forest Service, which manages the monument, urges the casual visitor to explore the downslope stretch rather than attempting the much more difficult upslope portion.

Free tours of Ape Cave are offered by the Forest Service, and you can rent lanterns for $3.00 at a concession stand at the entrance. If you don't care for dark, enclosed places, take a stroll on the nearby quarter-mile trail, where you will see tree molds created when lava surrounded the trees. The lava eventually decayed and disappeared, but the molds remain intact.

Although the crater is off-limits, you can climb to the rim from the south side on several trails. The most popular is Ptarmigan Trail, which has a 5,000-foot elevation gain and takes a long day for most hiker-climbers. Reservations are required.

For more information:

Mount St. Helens National Volcanic Monument,

Route 1, Box 369, Amboy, WA 98601. 206-247-5473; climbing hot line and reservations, 206-247-5800.

BIRD CREEK MEADOWS

Although businesses around Mount Adams complain that Puget Sounders hardly know that this part of Washington exists, the trade-off is that the area remains relatively uncrowded. Several wilderness areas surround Mount Adams, and areas open to vehicles have roads that dead-end at trails continuing on toward the mountain.

One of the most beautiful areas is Bird Creek Meadows, famous for the wildflower display that begins when the snow melts from the lowlands. The blossoms follow the melt line upward, so you'll find wildflowers there nearly all summer long. The peak is usually in July, but flowers of some kind bloom from May until the snow returns.

Bird Creek Meadows was more or less discovered by a naturalist named Wilhelm Suksdorf, who lived in a cabin near Laurel around the turn of the century and cataloged nearly 500 alpine plants and trees in the area. When the U.S. Forest Service was formed, it became involved in protecting the meadows and required cattlemen to build and maintain a drift fence below the meadows to keep sheep and cows out.

In 1972, the Yakima Nation expanded its boundaries to encompass about half of Mount Adams, including these meadows, but has left them open to hikers. The Yakimas keep a close watch on the area and charge an entry fee ($5.00 when this was written).

To reach the meadows, which are seventeen miles from Trout Lake, drive north of town about two miles toward Mount Adams Recreation Area. Turn right on Forest Service Road 82, which soon merges with Road 8290. When this road enters the Yakima Indian Reservation, it becomes Road 285. Continue past Mirror Lake to the trailhead parking area. The Bureau of Indian Affairs ranger will collect the use fee.

You have several choices of hikes from this trailhead. One of the most pleasant is a five-mile loop from Bird Lake that goes past several lakes and through the flower-strewn meadows.

For more information:

Gifford Pinchot National Forest, 6926 East Fourth Plain Boulevard, Vancouver, WA 98668-8944. 206-750-5000.

6 The Great Columbia Plain

GINKGO PETRIFIED FOREST STATE PARK

One of the state's most unusual parks is the Ginkgo, located along the Columbia River at Vantage. The park was created in 1934 with the purchase of the first tract of land containing rich exposures of petrified wood. Fossilized wood had been found in other parts of the Columbia Plain, but it wasn't until 1927, when the original highway between Ellensburg and Vantage was built, that the large number of fossils became apparent through the efforts of Professor George F. Beck at Central Washington State College in Ellensburg.

Polished specimens of petrified wood are on display in the interpretive center, and partially excavated petrified logs remain in their natural setting along the 2.5 miles of trails throughout the 6,000-acre park. More than 200 varieties of wood have been identified in the park, making it one of the most diverse such areas in the world.

The park gets its name from the ginkgo tree *(Ginkgo biloba)*, which is sometimes referred to as a "living fossil." It is the only survivor of a family of trees *(Ginkgoaceae)* that was once widely distributed across the temperate regions of both the Northern and Southern hemispheres. It made its first appearance more than 200 million years ago and is still used as an ornamental. It also is called the Sacred Tree of China, and its continued existence is largely due to its cultivation in Chinese temple gardens. It no longer exists in the wild anywhere in the world. Petrified ginkgo leaves are common, but petrified ginkgo logs are very unusual, which makes this park even more valuable.

The petrified forest was created by a chain of events that occurred over millions of years. Scientists have pieced together this scenario. About twenty million years ago, the Cascade Range did not yet exist, the Vantage area was very humid, and the land was covered with thick forests and dense underbrush. Then came great floods of molten lava from cracks and fissures in the earth's crust, eventually covering at least 200,000 square miles. In some places, the lava was more than 10,000 feet deep.

These eruptions created the Columbia Plateau, sometimes called the Great Columbia Plain. Over the centuries, soil was gradually created, and trees again grew in the region. Some died and fell into the lakes and swamps, becoming waterlogged and sinking into the mud and sediment. Once again, the area was covered with lava, and the submerged logs were sealed in an undamaged state. Over the following centuries, water seeped down through the lava. The water contained silica, which penetrated the logs and gradually replaced the wood, preserving its exact patterns. Some minerals carried along with the silica created the colors of the petrified logs.

After the Cascade Range was created by uplifts, the region became the arid, windy place we know today. The whole area gradually tipped toward the south, and erosion stripped away the lava, exposing the petrified forest.

The park is located a short distance west of I-90 at

Vantage. It has a three-quarter-mile interpretive loop trail that leads past several examples of petrified wood and plants. Another trail, more than two miles long, leads back into the sagebrush environment typical of the area.

For more information:

Ginkgo Petrified Forest State Park, Vantage, WA 98950. 509-856-2700.

COULEE DAM NATIONAL RECREATION AREA AND COLUMBIA BASIN PROJECT

Talk about the greening of America! The Columbia Basin Project, one of the few win-win dam projects in U.S. history, boasts more than 500,000 acres of crops where sand and tumbleweeds once blew. Another 87,000 acres are currently under consideration to be added to this immense garden for an eventual 1 million acres.

The Columbia Basin Project has completely changed the face of central Washington. The half million acres now "under water" (irrigated for cultivation) once were so dry that locals say a person had to be primed before he could spit. It was so barren, they say, that jackrabbits had to carry their lunch. The area still gets only a small amount of rainfall, but it has a long growing season – about 165 days – which made it desirable for the cultivation of crops. If only water could be found.

The project began with suggestions put forth in 1918 by the *Wenatchee World,* a local newspaper. In 1919, the state legislature appropriated funds to study the proposal. The idea remained alive, on both the state and national levels, until the 1930s, when President Franklin D. Roosevelt put the Grand Coulee Dam into his Public Works

Administration program. Thus, in the midst of the Great Depression, thousands of men were put to work building what was then the largest concrete structure in the world. The first power was generated in 1941, and the first irrigation canals were opened at the same time.

The dam created 150-mile-long Roosevelt Lake, which runs north into Canada. The lake quickly became a major recreational area, but the primary benefit of the dam, aside from electrical power, was the irrigation project. Although the Columbia River continues on its way downriver from the dam, running west for several miles before turning south in the area aptly called Big Bend Country, another system of waterways was created for the irrigation project.

Water from Roosevelt Lake was pumped into the dry Grand Coulee, which became a twenty-seven-mile-long holding area named Banks Lake. Dry Falls Dam was built at the south end of the coulee, and from here the water is sent out in canals, siphons, and tubes to the various irrigation districts. O'Sullivan Dam was built below Moses Lake to create the Potholes Reservoir, another holding area for water. The water flows south, both in man-made canals and along the contour of the land, until it returns to the Columbia River upstream from Pasco.

The irrigation project, under the direction of the U.S. Bureau of Reclamation, has had some unexpected benefits. The tilt of the land is southward, and the water filters down through the soil until it reaches an impenetrable layer of rock or hardpan. Then the water flows south until it reaches the Columbia River or the layer it follows comes close to the surface.

In many cases, the water rose to the surface and created lakes or new streams. Some of these lakes are now popular recreation areas. The Potholes Reservoir is a good example. The area was a hilly desert before the water began seeping in. Soon the area had hundreds of small desert islands poking up through the water. It became such a popular place to boat, fish, and camp that it was set aside as a recreation area, and a state park was created there.

Thus far, the project comprises some 2,300 miles of canals and laterals to distribute the water to about 6,000 farm units. It has had a positive effect on wildlife and recreation. Since its creation, more than thirty designated recreation areas, including picnic areas and overnight camping areas, have been added to the area, and more than two million people visit them each year. Fishermen catch trout, bass, sturgeons, walleyes, perch, whitefish, kokanees, and spiny rays, and ice fishing is a popular winter sport. Hunters go after waterfowl and upland game birds throughout the area.

Included in the project is the Columbia National Wildlife Refuge, a 233,100-acre patchwork of canals, lakes, and uplands south of O'Sullivan Dam and the Potholes Reservoir. Nearly all of the lakes in the refuge were created by the Columbia Basin Project and are called seep lakes. The nooks and crannies in the basaltic cliffs are used as nesting sites by red-tailed hawks, American kestrels, great horned owls, barn owls, ravens, and cliff swallows. California quail, black-crowned night herons, long-billed curlews, Chinese pheasants, northern harrier hawks, and American avocets also visit the area.

One of the most popular activities is simply watching water pour over the Grand Coulee Dam. Although the river seldom has so much water that the spillway is open all the time, the dam does release water from time to time for the benefit of visitors. The big show takes place each evening during the summer months. A sound and light show is held at the dam, with laser images projected on the dam or the water coming over the spillway.

For more information:

Coulee Dam National Recreation Area, P.O. Box 37, Coulee Dam, WA 99116. 509-633-9441.

Bureau of Reclamation, P.O. Box 815, Ephrata, WA 98823. 509-754-0200.

Columbia National Wildlife Refuge, P.O. Drawer F, Othello, WA 99344. 509-488-2668.

YAKIMA RIVER CANYON

Several years ago, when my children were young enough to think floating on inner tubes was a neat way to travel, I asked a river-runner friend if he thought the Yakima River between Ellensburg and Yakima would make a good weekend float trip.

"Who told you about the Yakima?" he demanded.

I understood why he was upset. He wanted to keep the place a secret. I felt the same way about Anacortes as a place to live and Rosario Beach at Deception Pass. We didn't make the trip, but since that time, the Yakima has become more and more popular. Not only do people float down it during the dog days of summer, but it also is popular with deer and bird hunters, fishermen, and bird-watchers. Bird watching has become so popular that the U.S. Bureau of Land Management recently published an elaborate brochure listing the birds that have been spotted in the twenty-four-mile river canyon.

As you drive through the area on I-82, you might consider the area nothing more than sparsely populated desert. However, the Bureau of Land Management's guide lists more than 200 species of birds. Twenty-one species of raptors alone have been seen here. Other types of birds include loons, grebes, cormorants, herons, waterfowl, vultures,

You're more likely to hear loons than to see them

game birds, rails, cranes, shorebirds, gulls, terns, doves, owls, goatsuckers, swifts, hummingbirds, kingfishers, woodpeckers, flycatchers, larks, swallows, corvids, chickadees, bushtits, nuthatches, creepers, wrens, dippers, kinglets, thrushes, thrashers, pipits, waxwings, shrikes, starlings, vireos, warblers, tanagers, grosbeaks, buntings, towhees, sparrows, blackbirds, orioles, and finches. Some barren wasteland!

Over the years, the river has been gradually developed for recreational boating. It offers several established campsites, toilets, boat launches, and even a footbridge across the river. The riverbank is a patchwork of public and private ownership, and you should obtain a map from the Bureau of Land Management that shows most of the property lines.

For more information:

U.S. Bureau of Land Management, 1133 North Western Avenue, Wenatchee, WA 98801. 509-662-4223.

OHME GARDENS

The high, arid, sun- and storm-blasted basaltic cliffs along the Columbia River are among the least likely places for a garden. But the view down the river to Wenatchee and beyond is terrific, and that is why Herman Ohme began his gardens here in 1929. He intended for them to be a cool, quiet family retreat, but the project got away from him. Within a decade, the gardens covered several acres and were growing, and people all over the area wanted to see them.

Ohme yielded and opened them to the public in 1939. He continued to expand them with additional plantings and new paths along the steep face of the cliff. The family planted thousands of evergreen trees, and where trees wouldn't grow, they planted low-growing alpine plants. They hauled in tons of rocks to build paths and retaining walls, pools, and waterfalls.

By the 1960s, the gardens had become something of a national institution. Newspapers and magazines published articles about them, and they became a stop on nearly every tour through the area. Today more than 30,000 travelers visit the gardens each year.

The gardens have been kept as natural in appearance as possible, using Cascade alpine meadows and Olympic rain forests as models. The evergreens are blended with rock formations to create natural effects. Stone pathways lead through small groves of trees, across open spaces, and past small pools with waterfalls draining them. An occasional shelter offers shade from the sun or the rare shower, and stone and wooden benches give visitors a place to sit and enjoy the views. Small mammals such as ground squirrels and rabbits wander at will, and songbirds stop in for a drink and a bath.

The gardens are three miles north of Wenatchee, near

the junction of US 2 and US 97. They are open daily from April 15 to October 15. An admission is charged.

For more information:

Ohme Gardens, 3327 Ohme Road, Wenatchee, WA 98801. 509-662-5785.

CHANNELED SCABLANDS DESERT LOOP

The Channeled Scablands are one of eastern Washington's most fascinating geological stories. Most geologists believe that the tortured landscape southwest of Spokane was created by a series of catastrophic floods during the Ice Age. These floods occurred when dams were created in western Montana by ice and debris, impounding water in huge lakes. When the ice melted, the dams broke, unleashing floods that swept down the Spokane River valley, across eastern Washington, and down to the Columbia River.

I-90 crosses the scablands, and as you drive south from Sprague, you'll cross many of the coulees and valleys created by the floods. You'll also see hundreds of the shiprocks left behind. These basaltic buttes are characterized by an almost identical shape: they all point in a general northeast-southwest direction, and the northeast end is sharper than the southwest point. Also, all of them have more soil on the southern end because the steady wind out of the southwest has gradually replaced the soil taken away by the floods. This southwest wind, bearing dust and soil from Oregon and California, has created the rich soil of the region.

The U.S. Bureau of Land Management and several state agencies have combined their resources to map out a 150-mile loop drive beginning at Ritzville on I-90 that shows off the Channeled Scablands and the wildlife that flourishes in the area. In Ritzville, take Marcellus Road north across Rocky Ford of Crab Creek (the lower portion of this creek is discussed in the section on Saddle Mountain and Crab Creek Coulee later in this chapter), where you can expect to see desert songbirds, waterfowl, and sometimes mule deer. Downstream a short distance is Crab Creek Canyon, a channel cut by the floods. The land is privately owned, and permission is required to enter it.

The route continues on to Coal Creek, which is on public land. State 28 is nearby, and the loop follows it

Sharp-tailed grouse

northeast to Harrington, where you turn left (west) on Seven Springs Road. This road goes through one of the last habitats of the Columbian sharp-tailed grouse. Don't miss the region's westernmost grove of ponderosa pine.

Pick up US 2 and continue west to Wilbur. Turn right onto Govan Road and follow it as it winds through a basaltic canyon that is lush with wildflowers and home to many species of birds. Migratory waterfowl use the canyon for nesting, and they attract bobcats, badgers, and coyotes.

Take State 21 south across Wilson Creek and Crab Creek to Lakeview Ranch, owned by the Bureau of Land Management. The ranch is one of the last habitats for sage grouse and is open for hiking and primitive camping. Trails lead out into Lake Creek Canyon, one of the most scenic spots in the area.

Follow State 21 through Odessa and back to I-90 fifteen miles west of Ritzville.

For more information:

Odessa Chamber of Commerce, P.O. Box 355, Odessa, WA 98159. 509-982-0049.

CONBOY LAKE NATIONAL WILDLIFE REFUGE

Conboy Lake, between Laurel and Glenwood, is actually more of a marsh than a lake, and like so many wetlands east of the Cascades, much of it was drained for crops by early farmers. The first 5,500 acres of a projected 10,000-acre refuge were acquired in 1964. Restoration of the lake and wildlife habitat has been limited, as most of the lake is still in private ownership.

In spite of this limitation, the refuge is one of the most beautiful places in the shadow of Mount Adams and the

Cascade Range. In February and March, waterfowl on their way north stop here to feed and rest. A few ducks and geese stay for the summer to nest among the flowering camas, and they are soon joined by snipes, sandhill cranes, and various songbirds.

By the end of summer, only a few of the lowest areas still hold water. Ranchers working the land under contract with the refuge cut Reed's canary grass, which was introduced to the refuge, and the native marsh grasses for hay. In the fall, the birds move south for the winter, completing the seasonal cycle.

The refuge, which is located thirty-five miles north of White Salmon in the Columbia Gorge, has a two-mile trail along the lakeshore and through the upland pine forest. Photographers particularly enjoy having Mount Adams as a backdrop.

For more information:

Conboy Lake National Wildlife Refuge, Box 5, Glenwood, WA 98619. 509-364-3410.

STEPTOE BUTTE

The Palouse Country is one of the Northwest's geological and agricultural treasures. These rolling hills are in the region south of Spokane and north of the Snake River. Their eastern boundary is in western Idaho, in the foothills of the Rocky Mountains. Their western boundary isn't so easy to define, but one thing is clear: The Palouse begins east of the Channeled Scablands. The scablands are lower in elevation, and it is elevation that has created the Palouse. Here the land is high enough to catch the clouds that have cleared the Cascades and swept across the dryland farming area.

The Palouse Country is among the best wheat-growing areas in the world. Never in the history of farming has the Palouse experienced a crop failure.

The Palouse is notable for its low but steep hills, which are covered with a thick layer of loess, soil deposited by winds over the centuries. In this case, the soil is brought in from Oregon by the steady wind out of the southwest. In some places, the soil is more than one hundred feet deep, and it has been enriched from time to time with fresh minerals from volcanic eruptions: Glacier Peak, Mazama (the Native American name for the peak that destroyed itself and created Crater Lake), and, more recently, Mount St. Helens.

Steptoe Butte State Park, at an elevation of 3,612 feet above sea level, protrudes 1,170 feet above the rich farmland below. It is a short distance east of the town of Steptoe on US 195 about 50 miles south of Spokane and 10 miles north of Colfax. From this pyramid-shaped peak, you can truly appreciate the beauty of the wheat fields below.

The peak has an unusual distinction. It is actually the top of a quartzite mountain more than 600 million years old, one of the northernmost peaks in the Selkirk Range, which was covered by basalt some 15 million years ago.

The peak was originally named Pyramid Peak but later was renamed in honor of Colonel Edward J. Steptoe, who was soundly defeated nearby on May 17, 1858, in a running battle with a large group of Native Americans. (In the geological vocabulary, any remnant of an older formation protruding out of a newer formation is now called a steptoe.) Some years later, an Englishman named James Davis bought a wagon in Walla Walla and headed north with his wife and children in search of a new home. After he turned down several opportunities to stop and claim land, his wife finally told him she was going no farther.

They were at a pleasant place with a grove of cottonwood trees and a year-round spring. There they set up housekeeping and opened a general store. They named the place Cottonwood Springs, but later on the town was renamed Cashup, because Davis told everyone the same thing: "Cash up front."

Davis built a hotel atop Steptoe Butte. It was a remarkable edifice with a wraparound balcony and furniture imported from England, and it was decorated with every kind of wheat grown in the area. The hotel became a popular retreat for people from Spokane and stood several years after Davis died in 1896. Finally, some young boys playing with matches accidentally burned it down.

The corkscrew road to the peak is always open, unless it is covered with snow or ice. Unfortunately, the summit is marred by several radio and television transmission towers. A modest state park at the base consists of two picnic tables and a well. It is maintained by Central Ferry State Park.

For more information:

Central Ferry State Park, 509-549-3551.

SADDLE MOUNTAIN AND CRAB CREEK VALLEY

Whoever invented the word *meandering* must have had Crab Creek in mind. This stream, never particularly large and sometimes almost a memory, has been officially designated as the longest creek in the United States.

It begins just outside Spokane and wanders across the Channeled Scablands, sometimes flowing north, other times south, but mostly west until it reaches the Grand Coulee area. There it swings south, then southeast, ambling back and forth until it at last reaches the base of Saddle

Mountain. For nearly twenty miles on, it tends to business and flows almost due west until it empties into the Columbia River near Beverly.

If you follow the creek from origin to mouth, you will see some of the most rugged landscape eastern Washington has to offer. The last twenty miles are among my favorite places in the state.

Crab Creek valley nestles against the dramatic face of Saddle Mountain. The floods that created the Channeled Scablands carved out the valley, leaving the eastern slopes of Saddle Mountain more gradual and less dramatic than the western face. The latter is spotted with wind-carved hoodoos and multicolored outcroppings that change colors according to the intensity of the sunlight. Most of the valley is under the protection of various state and federal wildlife agencies, although some land is owned by private hunting clubs and farmers.

The valley was settled after the Milwaukee Road built its electric railroad through the area in the early part of this century. All the other transcontinental railroads were already in place when the Milwaukee arrived, and it not only did not get the free land offered the pioneering railroads but it also got the most difficult landscape to traverse. The route through the lower Crab Creek valley was relatively tame, though, and two siding towns, Corfu and Smyrna, were established.

The Crab Creek Valley Road runs from Beverly on State 243 to State 26 near Othello. You can also drive to the summit of Saddle Mountain for sweeping views of the region. Drive south on State 243 from Beverly to Mattawa. Continue one mile east of Mattawa on the only road to "R" Road and turn left (west) on it to the dead end on Saddle Mountain.

For more information:

Washington Department of Wildlife, 509-754-4624.

Saddle Mountain National Wildlife Refuge, 735 East Main Street, Othello, WA 99344. 509-488-2668. (This refuge is inside the Hanford Nuclear Reservation and is closed to the public.)

7
The Okanogan and Northeast Corner

LITTLE PEND OREILLE WILDLIFE AREA

You probably won't be alone when you visit this 41,000-acre wildlife area; it is one of the most popular such areas in the state. Still, it is well worth visiting because of its natural beauty and the probability of seeing many kinds of wildlife.

The refuge is located on the western edge of the Selkirk Range thirteen miles southeast of Colville on State 20. Moose are gradually establishing themselves in northeast Washington, and you may spot one here. You also may see white-tailed and mule deer, beavers, black bears, blue and ruffed grouse, and lots of waterfowl. You can fish for rainbow, eastern brown, and cutthroat trout.

A network of roads covers nearly 200 miles of the refuge. The Watchable Wildlife Loop starts at the headquarters on State 20. The management urges visitors to carry in their own water and not to drive off the roads. Camping is permitted at eleven very primitive campgrounds. A map with their locations is available at the headquarters.

You might meet a moose

For more information:

Little Pend Oreille Wildlife Area, 1310 Bear Creek Road, Colville, WA 99114. 509-684-5343.

SALMO-PRIEST WILDERNESS AREA

This small wilderness area—just 63 acres shy of 40,000 acres—is tucked away in the far northeast corner of Washington. It borders Canada on the north and elbows its way over into Idaho. The saddlebag-shaped area is about ninety miles north of Spokane and is in the Selkirk Range. It is one of the few wilderness areas where backpacking has declined and horseback riding has increased substantially, but some of the more remote trails are still popular with hikers.

The wilderness was created in 1984 primarily because it is home to the dwindling mountain caribou herd that wanders through the area. It also hosts Washington's only known grizzly population, as well as wolverines, mountain goats, and possibly timber wolves. Deer, elk, coyotes, and black bears are abundant. Rocky Mountain bighorn sheep, cougars, a few moose, bobcats, lynx, martens, golden eagles, and Canadian lynx also inhabit the area. In addition, the Salmo River is a popular spot to fish for rainbow and cutthroat trout.

Salmo-Priest has about seventy-five miles of trails, the majority of which were built as fire trails. The major area that has no trails is in the Gypsy Ridge area. The most heavily traveled trails are the Salmo Loop and Shedroof Basin trails.

For more information:

Colville National Forest, 765 South Main Street, Colville, WA 99114. 509-684-3711.

CENTENNIAL TRAIL

It's amazing how forgiving our waterways are after we've treated them so badly. All over America, we see examples of streams, lakes, sounds, and canals that have come back after being ignored or abused. One example is the Spokane River, a relatively short river that flows from Lake Coeur d'Alene to the Columbia River. The Spokane has been important in the development of the Spokane–Coeur d'Alene area as a means of transportation and provider of power. The river was a mess until the Expo '74 World's Fair in Spokane, when the river, with its islands, rapids, and falls, was cleaned up and became the focal point of downtown Spokane.

The transformation was so dramatic that in 1986, a group of people developed another ambitious plan for the river: to preserve it from the Idaho state line, down the Spokane Valley, through the city of Spokane, and west to Riverside State Park. Idaho joined the project with plans to continue the Centennial Trail. It will start six or seven miles downlake from the town of Coeur d'Alene and continue through town and on to the Washington-Idaho border. This will make the trail about sixty-three miles long.

Eventually, it will be twelve feet wide, but the portion now complete is eight feet wide and paved. It is open only to nonmotorized traffic and is accessible to people with handicaps. It traverses several historic sites and parks and is near the museums in downtown Spokane. The trail is open from 6:30 A.M. to dusk year-round and can be entered anywhere in the heart of Spokane.

For more information:

Friends of the Centennial Trail, P.O. Box 351, Spokane, WA 99910-0351. 509-624-3450; group use permits: Riverside State Park, 509-456-2729 or 456-3964.

CAT TALES ENDANGERED SPECIES EDUCATION CENTER

Only recently opened, Cat Tales is an effort to protect several species of wildlife from extermination. To become a resident of the Cat Tales Endangered Species Education Center, the animal must be listed as endangered.

The center was created to provide a breeding center for endangered animals, but the public showed so much interest in the program that the founders decided to open it as an educational center, especially for children. One of the major points the center tries to get across is that wild animals, especially exotic ones, do not make good pets. Another message the center emphasizes is the importance of recycling and how we can take steps to preserve the earth.

Among the animals living in the center are two Bengal tigers, an African serval, a Patagonian puma, a Canadian puma, two California pumas, three tigers, two African lions, four leopards, two bobcats, and two Canadian lynx. Other large cats are expected, and some animals are borrowed from zoos around the country for the breeding program. Many of the animals have been confiscated from people who operate fly-by-night zoos and abuse the animals by beating them to get them angry and make them "more interesting" to customers.

The center's staff is licensed by the U.S. Department of Agriculture, and the center is a member of the American Association of Zookeepers. No admission is charged, but donations of $3.00 for adults and $2.00 for children are encouraged. Guided tours are offered upon request.

For more information:

Cat Tales Endangered Species Education Center,

17020 North Newport Highway, Mead, WA 99021. 509-238-4126.

RIVERSIDE STATE PARK: LITTLE SPOKANE RIVER NATURAL AREA

Riverside State Park has long been one of the nicest green places in the Spokane Valley. It is one of the states larger parks – 7,655 acres along nearly eight miles of the Spokane River. In addition to having the Spokane River and Deep Creek flowing through it, the park has large basaltic rock formations and thick conifer forests.

Recently, several miles of the Little Spokane River

Bald eagle fishermen

were added to the park. A 6-mile trail follows the riverbank, and a 3.5-mile canoe route has been marked.

In the Little Spokane River Natural Area, the river flows slowly, enabling both walkers and paddlers to enjoy the beauty of the area. You can expect to see several species of songbirds in the tall cottonwoods and dense brush along the riverbank. Great blue herons and ospreys roost along the river, and bald eagles sometimes winter over here. Beavers, muskrat, white-tailed deer, coyotes, and porcupines also wander through.

The canoe put-in is at the Spokane Trout Hatchery at the end of Waikiki Road, and the take-out is at the mouth of the river where it empties into the Spokane River off State 291.

For more information:

Riverside State Park, 509-456-3964.

TURNBULL NATIONAL WILDLIFE REFUGE

One legacy of the great Spokane floods that created the Channeled Scablands was a large number of small, usually shallow lakes south of Spokane. Some were seasonal, but many were not. Over the years, as farmland became more scarce, many of the lakes were drained and turned into fields.

This, of course, deprived waterfowl of their habitat, and their numbers declined dramatically. In an effort to reverse this trend, the 15,468-acre Turnbull National Wildlife Refuge was created in 1937. It is located 4 miles south of Cheney on Cheney-Plaza Road, in the heart of the Channeled Scablands lake district.

The management set about restoring the lakes and

marshes that had been drained, and the refuge soon became a prime nesting area for waterfowl on the Pacific flyway. Up to 50,000 birds have been counted there during the fall migration. The area attracts large numbers of ducks, geese, and swans. It is best known for its large population of diving ducks, such as redheads, canvasbacks, and scaup.

In addition to the waterfowl, virtually every kind of songbird and upland game bird found in the Great Columbia Plain can be seen at the refuge at one time or another. Bird-watchers have recorded more than 200 species here. The refuge also supports a large mammal population, including elk, white-tailed deer, coyotes, badgers, porcupines, beavers, and muskrat. Smaller mammals, such as chipmunks, red squirrels, and Columbian ground squirrels, also are common.

Canada goslings

An auto route takes you through the refuge, with several short trails leading off from the parking areas. This is a good place for photography because the weather is usually clear.

For more information:

Turnbull National Wildlife Refuge, South 26010 Smith Road, Cheney, WA 99004. 509-235-4723.

8
The San Juan Islands

It would take an extremely blasé person to take a ride on Washington State Ferry from Anacortes to the San Juan Islands and not be impressed with the scenery. With only a bit of immodesty, the state calls it the most beautiful ferry ride in America; Alaskans might insist that the statement be toned down by limiting the claim to the Lower 48.

Departing the dock at Anacortes does give the definite sense of embarking on a voyage, and no matter what kind of weather is in effect, the rails on the outside decks are always crowded with people, much as a cruise ship is when it departs. Ahead lie the hilly, green-and-brown islands, most of which still have far more trees than houses and people. Sometimes the channel the ferry must follow is only a stone's throw from the islands.

Left behind on the mainland is the perpetual roar of I-5, the suburbs that cover more and more rich farmland each year, and the tension that seems to be part of the American experience. In fact, you can watch tension gradually leave ferry passengers as the trip progresses. By the time the ferry reaches the first stop on Lopez Island, most people are well on their way to being rested.

The San Juan Islands have always been a place apart,

even though they are relatively close to the mainland. They have always had a foreign-destinatioin air to them, in part because each of the larger inhabited islands had its own personality. Speaking in generalities, the islanders are private by nature or they wouldn't be there, and they have a nationalistic attitude toward the island of their choice.

As an example, I once asked a woman on Orcas Island if she had known the late novelist Charlotte Paul. "No," the woman answered reasonably. "She lived on Lopez Island." And Charlotte Paul told me that a bank serving the islands established a scholarship for students from the islands, but that not one student who won the scholarship to that time, which was in the 1970s, had remained in college. Every one quit school and came home for the security of the islands.

The state ferry calls on only four of the 200-plus islands: Lopez, Shaw, Orcas, and San Juan. Shaw is so sparsely populated that it probably wouldn't have ferry service if it weren't almost jammed up against Orcas Island. Several of the other islands are inhabited, but they rely on a small inter-island airline or their own resources to get on and off the islands. They don't want ferry service bringing the hordes of tourists that have changed the character of the other islands. Not surprisingly, many who live on the islands not served by state ferries are wealthy and own their own planes.

The islands are part of a large archipelago of mountain tops rising out of the saltwater between the United States and Canada. The entire Inside Passage to Alaska, which runs from Olympia, Washington, along the Canadian coast to Skagway, Alaska, consists of thousands of islands claimed by both nations, but the San Juans are part of a group that includes Canada's Gulf Islands. The San Juans and Gulf Islands are separated only by that imaginary line that divides the two countries. In addition to the four main islands—Lopez, Shaw, Orcas, and San Juan—the group also includes Blakely, Decatur, Stuart, Waldron, and a scattering of smaller islands, some inhabited, some not: Wasp, Jones, Spieden, Matia, Sucia, and Patos, for example. Others nearby that aren't always shown on the San Juan list but probably should be are Guemes Island, a residential island just off Anacortes; rocky Cypress Island, between Guemes and Blakely islands; Sinclair and Vendovi islands north of Cypress and Guemes, both of which are privately owned, and Lummi Island, just off the mainland near Bellingham.

It is possible to visit all the islands if you are traveling by boat, which is one of the most popular and practical ways of getting around the archipelago. It will be a rare visit to the islands when you don't meet someone who arrived there by sailboat, frequently from California. They liked what they saw and stayed. For all of California's great sailing weather, it has virtually no sheltered waters and precious few islands.

After you have visited each of the islands, you will probably go home with each island represented in your memory by a scene or an incident you experienced. And you will be surprised at the physical diversity among the islands, even though they are so close together. You can visit a virtual rain forest on Orcas Island, yet walk among cacti on Lopez and San Juan.

My favorite memories of Lopez, where I have spent the most time, involve the week my family and I spent in a beach shack on Madkeye Harbor. There's no better word to describe our quarters; the shack belonged to a high school teacher in Seattle to whom it had been willed by an old friend with whom he spent several weekends. In turn, the teacher let people use it free of charge if they met his rather casual criteria. The four children, their mother, and

I slept on primitive bunks and beds, ate from battered pots and pans, and we had a wonderful time.

The other perfect memory comes from a visit many years later, after the children were grown and I was traveling alone again. I went to Lopez for a quick look around, drove to Fisherman Bay and saw the most perfect morning the bay had ever offered. The sun was out, no clouds in the sky, not a hint of a breeze, and all the fishing boats and sailboats were reflected perfect in the calm water. The sky and water were blue, and it looked as if every boat had a fresh coat of paint. Perfection.

Lopez has long been a favorite with bicyclists because it has the fewest hills of any major island. It isn't as flat as western Kansas, but it comes close. It is still mostly rural, in spite of houses that are gradually building a ring around the rocky headlands and tiny islets offshore.

Odlin County Park near the ferry landing has camping, picnic sites, a boat ramp, and a good beach for wading or swimming, if you can bear the cold water. Spencer Spit State Park has the same amenities, and Fisherman Bay has camping as well. Lopez also has a scattering of motels and bed and breakfasts, but it is less developed than San Juan and Orcas Islands.

Orcas Island is the largest of the San Juans and also has the highest mountains. It is oddly shaped with two sounds, reasonably but unimaginatively named West and East Sounds, that almost cut the island into three sections. The island has one or two popular resorts, several hotels, country inns, and bed and breakfasts. Discover Moran State Park, nearly 5,000 acres of mountains, lakes, forests, and trails. It is the fourth largest of the state's parks and one of the most popular. It has many campsites, some 30 miles of hiking trails and lots of silence.

The park surrounds Mount Constitution, at 2,428 feet

the highest point in the islands. No first-time visitor to the islands should miss the opportunity to drive to the summit for the 360-degree view that reveals nearly every island in both the United States and Canada, plus the major volcanoes, from Mount Baker south to Mount St. Helens. The drive winds through thick forest, and perched on the summit is a stone tower built by the Civilian Conservation Corps in 1936. It was designed by the noted architect Ellsworth Storey and patterned after watchtowers in the Caucasus Mountains of Eastern Europe. Stairs lead to the top of the tower for the best view. Unfortunately, the tower shares the summit with television and radio transmission towers, which are like blemishes on a beautiful face.

Shaw is the smallest island served by ferries and has the least to offer tourists. Unless you are fortunate enough to secure one of the few campsites in Shaw Island County Park or have a boat, plan to arrive early in the day, drive or bike around the island, and catch a ferry off the island later in the day.

San Juan Island is the busiest of the islands, and since it is the county seat it has more briefcases than all the others combined. San Juan also has some of the most interesting historical sites. Of international significance, more or less, is the San Juan Historical Park, which consists of English Camp and American Camp on the western side of the island.

The park commemorates a close call the United States had with England in 1859. The Treaty of 1846 established the international boundary between Canada and the United States at the 49th Parallel, but left unresolved was the boundary between Vancouver Island and the United States. The cluster of islands that make up Canada's Gulf Islands and the United States' San Juan Islands was ignored in the treaty. The Hudson Bay Company claimed them, but

Americans kept showing up in the islands and staking claims, ignoring the British.

The issue finally came to a head when an American settler named Lyman Cutler (or Cutlar) shot a British pig that had been rooting in his potato patch. He was especially upset because he had rowed forty miles round trip to the mainland to buy those seed potatoes.

It was a shot heard 'round the world. Tempers flared and things became very tense. The British sent troops to their encampment at English Bay, and the Americans sent soldiers such as Captain George Pickett serving under General Winfield Scott. Pickett and the other American soldiers were stationed on the southern end of San Juan Island, a windswept, barren place that bore no resemblance to the cozy little cove with tall oak trees where the British were bivouacked. The opportunity for an all-out war definitely existed, and the feud simmered for several years, until the boundary issue was at last settled in 1871 by a panel of judges appointed by Germany's Kaiser Wilhelm after a joint high commission called by the United States and Britain had asked him to intercede. The judges selected Haro Strait as the international boundary.

Today the situation is commemorated by the San Juan National Historic Park. English Camp still has buildings dating back to the English period, including a picturesque log blockhouse standing near the beach. All buildings are open to visitors. American Camp isn't so inviting. As noted earlier, it is on the barren and windswept southern end of the island, and its most notable feature is the thousands of rabbits that live in a maze of underground warrens. They are a legacy of a settler's plan to bring a food supply to the island. The plan worked better than anyone would have wanted.

San Juan is also noted for the family or pod of killer

whales, Orcas, that cruises the waters around the island, particularly along the west coast. It is common to see them from the beach or bluffs overlooking the ocean, and if you are lucky enough to be in a small boat when they come by, you may get to see the massive creatures almost eyeball-to-eyeball. Once my family and I were fishing for salmon off the island in a twenty-two-foot boat when the orcas joined us. All around us fishermen were cursing and gnashing their teeth because when orcas appear, salmon wisely disappear. Orcas like salmon almost as much as we do.

Sometimes other whales come into the area, particularly the minke and grays who migrate back and fourth between Alaska and the Sea of Cortez. The Whale Museum in Friday Harbor, San Juan Island, has exhibits on the great beasts.

The state owns four small groups of islands off the northern shore of Orcas Island: Patos, Sucia, Matia, and Clark. These two dozen islands were originally owned by the federal government and set aside as part of a coastal defense system. When the system became obsolete, the islands were turned over to the state and private developers, but became public property when groups were formed to preserve them as both state parks and wilderness area. All can be reached only by boat or seaplane.

Patos Island State Park covers almost the entire island; only a couple of acres is set aside for the Coast Guard's automated Patos Lighthouse.

Sucia Islands is a group of granite fingers with sheltered bays, making them one of the most popular marine parks in the state. The park covers 562 acres. The islands have many hiking trails and cozy little bays for mooring boats or camping on shore.

Matia Island has a small park of only five acres and

the rest of the island is a National Wildlife Refuge. It has several trails and a good anchorage for boaters.

The Clark Island group is similar with a fifty-six-acre park. The island has no fresh water so it isn't heavily visited.

For more information:

Odlin County Park, Lopez Island. 360-468-2496.

Spencer Spit State Park, Lopez Island. 360-468-2251.

Moran State Park, Orcas Island. 360-376-2326.

San Juan National Historical Park, San Juan Island. 360-378-2240.

Matia, Sucia, Patos, and Clark Island parks are administered by the Lime Kiln Point State Park, Friday Harbor, San Juan Island. 360-378-2044.

Appendix

Washington's State Bird
Willow goldfinch

Washington's State Flower
Coast rhododendron

Washington's State Tree
Western hemlock

WASHINGTON'S ENDANGERED AND THREATENED WILDLIFE SPECIES

An *endangered* species is in immediate danger of extinction in all or a large part of its range. A *threatened* species is in slightly better shape but may become endangered in all or a large part of its range. *Extinction* of a species is the complete elimination of the species from the face of the earth. *Extirpation* is the elimination of a species from portions of its former range.

Endangered Animals

Leatherback sea turtle, American white pelican, brown pelican, peregrine falcon, sandhill crane, upland sandpiper, spotted owl, sperm whale, gray whale, finback whale, sei whale, humpback whale, right whale, gray wolf, grizzly bear, sea otter, Columbia white-tailed deer, mountain caribou.

Threatened Animals

Aleutian Canada goose, bald eagle, grizzly bear, Oregon silverspot butterfly, western pond turtle, green sea turtle, western snowy plover, loggerhead sea turtle, ferruginous hawk, bald eagle, pygmy rabbit.

Threatened Plants

Rose-purple sand verbena, Blue Mountain onion, northern wormwood, white-topped aster, Jessica's aster, Cotton's milk vetch, Columbia milk vetch, transparent milk vetch, whited milk vetch, Thurber's reed grass, reed grass, broad-fruit mariposa, obscure Indian paintbrush, golden paintbrush, Clackamas corydalis, pale larkspur, Wenatchee larkspur, basalt daisy, Howell's fleabane, showy stickseed, Palouse goldenweed, Howellia, smooth desert parsley, Suksdorf's desert parsley, Hoover's desert parsley, Cusick's lupine, bank monkey flower, stalk-leaved monkey flower, Washington's monkey flower, Howell's montia, Barrett's beardtongue, Chelan rock mat, sticky phacelia, sea cliff bluegrass, Washington polemonium, obscure buttercup, Columbia yellow cress, northwest raspberry, Oregon checker-mallow, Seely's silene, Spalding's silene, pale blue-eyed grass, Oregon sullivantia, Hoover's tauschia, Thompson's clover.

TRAIL TERMINOLOGY

The U.S. Forest Service offers these three categories of hiking trails:

Easy: Free of obstacles, grades of 10 percent or less, safe and well-marked trails

Moderate: May have roots and embedded rocks on the trail and sustained grades up to 20 percent

Difficult: Roots, embedded rocks, and other obstacles and sustained grades up to 30 percent

As a general rule, allow thirty minutes for each mile hiked.

TEN ESSENTIALS FOR HIKERS

Extra clothing
Extra food
Sunglasses
Knife
Firestarter
First-aid kit
Matches in a waterproof container
Flashlight with alkaline batteries
Map
Compass

TEN ESSENTIALS FOR A DAY TRIP

Map and compass

Flashlight with alkaline batteries

Matches, candle, or firestarter; be sure matches are protected

Small knife

First-aid kit; include items for blisters and headaches

Sunglasses, sunscreen, and mosquito repellent

Mirror and whistle

Rain gear and extra clothing

Water (at least a quart)

Extra food (high-energy snack such as candy, jerky, or meat bars)

WHITE-WATER RATINGS

Class 1: Easy.

Class 2: Moderate.

Class 3: Dangerous; novices should consider lining or portaging boats.

Class 4: Very dangerous; novices should line or portage boats.

Class 5: Extremely dangerous; even experts should consider portaging.

Class 6: Unrunnable; portage boats.

AVOIDING HYPOTHERMIA

Nearly every year, someone dies of hypothermia in Washington, and it isn't only in winter. Hypothermia is one of the leading causes of deaths during the summer months. A common scenario goes like this: A group goes on a day hike in the mountains. Rain begins to fall and the wind is blowing. Someone in the group doesn't have rain gear and isn't able to get dry and warm. That person begins shivering uncontrollably, becomes disoriented, falls asleep, and never wakes up.

Avoiding hypothermia should be a top priority while enjoying the outdoors, and the way to do so is simple: Stay dry and out of the wind. Take clothing suitable for the worst weather expected, which means rain gear and spare warm socks, shirt, and pants. If you are unable to stay dry and warm, get out of the wind, build a fire, and make a warm drink. If you don't have the proper clothing and can't build a suitable shelter, keep moving to generate body heat.

ESSENTIALS FOR WINTER TRAVEL

Always tell a friend or family member exactly where you are going. It's a good idea to mark your route on a map and leave it with that person. Always call him or her when you return. Take the following items:

Topographic map and compass

Flashlight and spare batteries

Matches, firestarter, and good knife

Extra food and water

Ski or snowshoe repair kit

Wool or synthetic clothing that will wick moisture while retaining its insulating properties

Change of clothes

Waterproof parka and rain pants

Ground insulation, preferably a closed-cell foam pad that will keep you off the snow

First-aid kit, sunglasses, and sunscreen

Avalanche rescue beacons, avalanche probes, and shovels if you are traveling in avalanche terrain

NORDIC SKI TRAIL ETIQUETTE

When skiing in a track, give the downhill skier the right of way.

Do not go on cross-country tracks with snowmobiles and snowshoes because they damage the tracks.

Ask permission before entering private property.

Pack out all trash, even fruit peels.

Avoid disturbing wild animals. Stay out of known elk and deer wintering areas. If you see a wild animal, quietly detour around it.

Stay well away from established travel routes for personal sanitary needs.

WALKING SOFTLY

Keep your group small. Large groups tend to multiply damage to the wilderness, and they can be disruptive to others. Groups entering a designated wilderness area must be no larger than twelve people and twelve head of stock.

"In years past we spoke of wilderness survival as the ability of people to survive the wilderness. Now we speak of wilderness survival as the land's ability to survive people." This statement by the U.S. Forest Service sums up the problem of people and wilderness throughout the world, and each of us can reduce the human impact on wilderness by using common sense and common courtesy. This approach is called the "No Trace" technique and includes these rules:

Stay on designated trails, never shortcut switchbacks.

When traveling cross-country, spread out and try to avoid wet meadows and fragile areas.

Never mark or blaze your route. Let others experience the challenge of finding their way as you did.

When meeting horses on the trail, step to the lower side of trail to allow them to pass.

When Camping

Avoid open areas and select well-drained sites away from water and trails.

Mule deer

Choose well-established campsites if you must use popular areas.

Avoid trenching around tents. Some areas have special setback regulations to prevent damage.

Avoid building campfires. Many high-use areas suffer

from the effects of campfires and wood gathering. Use a lightweight cookstove instead of a fire.

If you must have a campfire:

Use an existing fire ring unless you are near water or a trail. Keep your fire small. Burn only small sticks that can be broken by hand. (Leave your ax and saw at home.)

Never cut live trees or dead snags.

Do not build fires within one hundred feet of lakes, streams, or trails (all wildernesses). Some areas have special campfire setbacks.

Never leave a fire unattended, and make sure your fire is dead before you leave.

Pack out all plastic, foil, and glass. Don't try to burn it.

Sanitation

Bathe and wash 200 feet from all water sources.

Use only small amounts of biodegradable soap for washing.

Bury human waste 200 feet from water in a "cat hole" no more than 8 inches deep.

Bury fish entrails using the "cat hole" method. Never throw them into lakes or streams.

Never bury trash; animals dig it up.

Pack it in, pack it out. Don't leave litter behind.

Backcountry Courtesy

Keep the noise level down. Leave radios and tape players at home.

Keep pets under control at all times.

Never pick wildflowers or hack on trees or shrubs.

Never shoot firearms around lakes, streams, trails, or campsites.

Take only pictures. Leave with only fond memories.

TIPS FOR VIEWING WILDLIFE

Be quiet. Quick movements and loud noises scare birds and animals. Your car or boat is a good blind, and you may see more by remaining in the vehicle.

Be patient. Entering an area by car, by boat, or on foot may initially disturb birds and animals, but usually they will return if they don't feel threatened.

Visiting too many sites in one day may be disappointing, so allow plenty of time for each visit.

Take binoculars or spotting scopes so you can see better from a distance.

Use field guides to help identify wildlife. Most refuges also have a checklist of species common to the area.

Take a trip with a naturalist or professional wildlife guide. He or she knows the area and can help you spot the wildlife there.

Respect wildlife and try to avoid disturbing it. Birds and animals will stay only in areas they feel secure.

Don't feed or try to pet wildlife.

Avoid nesting areas in the spring.

Stay within designated areas to avoid disturbing wildlife or wandering onto private land.

Don't remove plants or animals.

Resources

Bureau of Reclamation, P.O. Box 815, Ephrata, WA 98823. 509-754-0200.

Camas-Washougal Chamber of Commerce, 422 N.E. Fourth Avenue, Camas, WA 98607. 206-834-2472.

Columbia National Wildlife Refuge, P.O. Drawer F, Othello, WA 99344. 509-488-2668.

Columbia River Gorge National Scenic Area, 902 Wasco Avenue, Suite 200, Hood River, OR 97031. 503-386-2333.

Conboy Lake National Wildlife Refuge, Box 5, Glenwood, WA 98619. 509-364-3410.

Coulee Dam National Recreation Area, P.O. Box 37, Coulee Dam, WA 99116. 509-633-9441.

Friends of the Centennial Trail, P.O. Box 351, Spokane, WA 99910-0351. 509-624-3450. Group use permits: Riverside State Park, 509-456-2729 or 456-3964.

Gifford Pinchot National Forest, 6926 East Fourth Plain Boulevard, Vancouver, WA 98668-8944. 206-750-5000.

Ginkgo Petrified Forest State Park, Vantage, WA 98950. 509-856-2700.

Grays Harbor Chamber of Commerce, 506 Duffy Street, Aberdeen, WA 98520. 206-532-1924.

Grays Harbor National Wildlife Refuge, c/o Nisqually National Wildlife Refuge, 100 Brown Farm Road, Olympia, WA 98506. 206-753-9467.

Julia Butler Hansen National Wildlife Refuge, P.O. Box 566, Cathlamet, WA 98612. 206-795-3915.

Klickitat County Tourism Committee, P.O. Box 1220, Goldendale, WA 98620. 509-773-3466.

Little Pend Oreille Wildlife Area, 1310 Bear Creek Road, Colville, WA 99114. 509-684-5343.

Mount Adams Chamber of Commerce, P.O. Box 449, White Salmon, WA 98672. 509-493-3630.

Mount Baker–Snoqualmie National Forest 21905 Sixty-fourth Avenue West, Mountlake Terrace, WA 98043. 206-775-9702.

Mount Rainier National Park, Ashford, WA 98304. 206-569-2211.

Mount Vernon Chamber of Commerce, 325 East College Way, Mount Vernon, WA 98273. 800-428-8547 (42-TULIP).

North Cascades National Park, 800 State Street, Sedro Woolley, WA 98284. 206-856-5700.

Northwest Trek Wildlife Park, 11610 Trek Drive East, Eatonville, WA 98328. 206-847-1901.

Oak Creek Wildlife Area, 16601 Highway 12, Naches, WA 98937. 509-653-2390.

Ohme Gardens, 3327 Ohme Road, Wenatchee, WA 98801. 509-662-5785.

Olympic National Park, 600 East Park Avenue, Port Angeles, WA 98362. 206-452-4501.

Point Defiance Zoo and Aquarium, 5400 North Pearl Street, Tacoma, WA 98407-5337. 206-591-5335.

Ridgefield National Wildlife Refuge, 301 North Third Street, Ridgefield, WA 98642. 206-887-4106.

San Juan Islands National Wildlife Refuge, c/o Nisqually National Wildlife Reserve Complex, 100 Brown Farm Road, Olympia, WA 98506. 206-753-9467.

Skagit Wildlife Area, 2214 Wylie Road, Mount Vernon, WA 98273. 206-445-4441.

Skamania County Chamber of Commerce, P.O. Box 1037, Stevenson, WA 98648. 509-427-8911.

Turnbull National Wildlife Refuge, South 26010 Smith Road, Cheney, WA 99004. 509-235-4723.

Washington Department of Wildlife, 600 Capitol Way North, Olympia, WA 98501-1091. 206-753-5707.

Wenatchee National Forest, 301 Yakima Street, Wenatchee, WA 98807-0811. 509-662-4335.

Willapa National Wildlife Refuge, HC 01 Box 910, Ilwaco, WA 98624. 206-484-3482.

Wolf Haven, 3111 Offut Lake Road, Tenino, WA 98589. 206-264-4695.

Woodland Park Zoological Gardens, 5500 Phinney Avenue North, Seattle, WA 98103-5897. 206-684-4800.

Bibliography

La Tourrette, Joe. *Washington Wildlife Viewing Guide.* Helena and Billings, Mont.: Falcon Press, 1992.

McCoy, Keith, and Darryl Lloyd. *Columbia Gorge Magazine* 2 (Summer 1991), "Bird Creek Meadows."

Schaffer, Jeffrey P., and Andy Selters. *The Pacific Crest Trail.* Vols. 1 and 2. Berkeley: Wilderness Press, 1990.

Scott, James W., and Melly A. Reuling. *Washington Public Shore Guide–Marine Waters.* Seattle: Department of Ecology and University of Washington Press, 1986.

Springer, Michael, comp. *The Columbia Gorge:* A Unique American Treasure. Pullman, Wash.: Washington State University Cooperative Extension Service, 1984.

Index